Spirit
of Place

Spirit of Place

The Roadside Shrines of Poland

Sophie Hodorowicz Knab

Hippocrene Books, Inc.
New York

Also by Sophie Hodorowicz Knab:

Polish Customs, Traditions and Folklore

The Polish Country Kitchen Cookbook

Polish Herbs, Flowers & Folk Medicine

*Wearing the Letter P: Polish Women as Forced
Laborers in Nazi Germany, 1939-1945*

*Naznaczone Literą "P" Polki jak robotnice przymusowe
w III Rzeszy 1939-1945*

Interior design by K & P Publishing/Barbara Keane-Pigeon.

Except where otherwise noted, all photos are taken by Edward J. Knab.

For further information, contact:
Hippocrene Books, Inc.
171 Madison Avenue
New York, NY 10016
www.hippocrenebooks.com

ISBN: 978-0-7818-1434-8

Cataloging-in-Publication Data is available from the Library of Congress.

Printed in the United States of America.

DEDICATION

*This book is dedicated to the keepers of the shrines,
past, present, and future*

CONTENTS

ACKNOWLEDGEMENTS

In Poland:

First and foremost to Krystyna Bartosik, who I met in Poland in 1993 and has been an unflagging advocate of whatever book I have been working on over these many decades including this one; Michał Zalewski for his very generous permission to use whatever photos and information I needed from his website kapliczki.org.pl when the pandemic prevented further travel and photography in Poland; my Zalewski family who are with me in all my endeavors but especially Jadwiga and Krzysztof Stańczyk; the Muzeum Etnograficzne im. Seweryna Udzieli w Krakowie and Gregorz Graff and Justyna Masłowiec in particular; Magdalena Bednarska of the website polskaniezwykla.pl who so graciously acted as an intermediary between myself and the artists and photographers of roadside shrines in Poland; Radosław Płużek from Portal Sucha at suchainfo. pl; the Facebook group Region Szamotulski-portal kulturalno-historyczny w Duznikach; Radosław Nowek and Krzysztof Woźniak of konskie.org.pl and photographers Krzysztof Urbański; Marian Dąbkowski.

In America:

My husband's uncle and godfather, Edward J. Knab, would say to me, "I'm going to the Shrine at Our Lady of Fatima and pray that your book gets published." Uncle Ed, I wish you were here so I could tell you that your prayers were heard and to tell you how grateful I am.

My heartfelt thanks to Jan Filipiak, Rev. Czesław Krysa, Diane and Steve Woloszyn, Andrew Golebiowski; Frank and Judy Krauza; Carla Hazard Tomaszewski, Edith and Claire Pula; Rev. Charles Jan Di Mascola; Beth Saunders and Lindsey Loeper at the Special Collections, University of Maryland, Baltimore County; the Wilno Heritage Society. I also wish to recognize all the libraries throughout the United States who lend their books in Polish so that we may research and write, as well as all the writers, photographers, and artists who so generously contribute and share their creative work on Wikipedia in English and in Polish for the world to access and utilize freely.

Thanks to Edward Knab, husband, photographer, consultant, cheerleader, and, oftentimes, therapist when I start losing it.

Thanks also to Priti Gress, editor at Hippocrene Books and Barbara Keane-Pigeon, production manager, and all the people at Hippocrene Books, Inc. who I never get to meet but who work behind the scenes to bring my books into existence—my deepest gratitude.

INTRODUCTION

It is said that every country has its own genius loci, its "spirit of place," meaning that particular characteristic that makes it distinctive. Holland has tulips and windmills, Egypt has the pyramids, and Italy its Roman architecture. For Poland, that spirit of place, that special individuality that marks it, must be the tens of thousands of roadside chapels, crosses, and shrines that dot both its cityscape and landscape.

Anyone who has traveled to Poland has to agree that it is impossible not to notice the innumerable crosses, religious statues, and little chapels that seem to be everywhere one looks. Enter a courtyard in Warsaw or Kraków and discover a statue of the Blessed Virgin Mary mounted on a pedestal with fresh flowers at her feet. Walk down a city sidewalk and there's a figure of St. Florian or of the Holy Family. Driving through a small town, a niche under the eaves of a home contains a figure of the Sacred Heart of Jesus. Nailed to a tree is a little open wooden box with a small image of Our Lady of Częstochowa. Quite by accident you may spy a tall wooden cross hidden in the woods, just off the beaten path, or see one standing alone and majestic in an open meadow. They are simply everywhere. Some are of a size that denote power and substance. Some are so small as to evoke a sense of humility. Some are threadbare and worn, yet emit an aura of permanence and timelessness. All of them seem to blend in harmoniously with the environment and beautify it. What are these objects? What do they mean? How did they come to be here, in this particular place? Who set them here? Why are they important?

Sociologists would call the hundreds of thousands of small chapels, crosses, and holy figures seen throughout Poland part of the material culture of a country. That is, they are physical objects in an environment that can be seen and touched. More importantly, these objects are also a symbol of something unseen, something that can't

Photo left: *Świniary in southern Poland, erected in 1958.*

be physically touched that comes from within the humans themselves—a feeling or an emotion that motivates people to create them in the first place. That something from within, that something internal that made manifest the roadside shrines on the landscape of Poland, was the Catholic faith. Desiring to translate their spiritual thoughts, feelings, and experiences into something material, something tangible, the people of Poland built magnificent churches as well as the innumerable chapels, crosses, and statues across their entire land, right down to the smallest village in the most remote locations. A thousand years of Christianity left its mark on the landscape of Poland like no other.

The landscape of any country, however, is a complex whole that can tell us much about the humans that live there. It is humans who shape, create, and transform their environment as they live, work, play, dream, and die across the generations. Every object in the landscape also has a story to tell and the shrines and chapels of Poland are no different. Whether carved in wood or chiseled in stone, whether funded by the clergy, the very wealthy, or the poorest man in the smallest village, the roadside shrines are also more than the expression of their faith. They are a country's way of life. They are works of art that speak to the creative spirit that once stirred within a heart to carve a statue, to gather stones to build a foundation, or inspired someone to gather words to form a poem or mix colors for a painting. They are messages from the past that reveal what at one time was important to this person, to this village, to a city block. They speak of personal and community joys as well as worries and the events and history that took place within their lifetime. They are a legacy inscribed on the landscape by the people of Poland as a way for future generations to come to know them and to remember them. They are indicative of the personality of Poland—all those innumerable qualities that reflect the struggle of a land and its people to be itself—its very spirit.

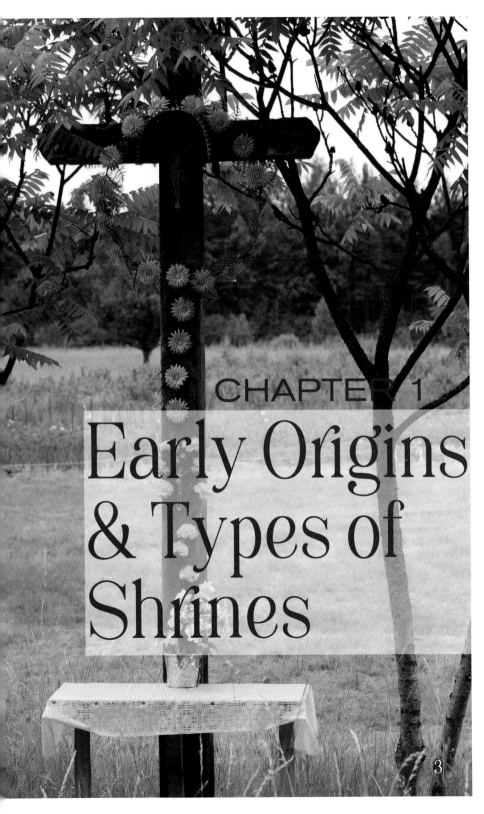

CHAPTER 1

Early Origins
& Types of
Shrines

Ever since its acceptance of Christianity in 966 AD, Poland as a country has survived on the strength of its faith. When Jan Sobieski fought the Turks at Vienna in 1683, he entrusted his kingdom to the protection of the Blessed Virgin Mary and saved Europe from Muslim domination. When Poland was partitioned by Austria, Prussia, and Russia and ceased to exist as a country on the maps of Europe for one hundred twenty-three years, the people learned their prayers in secret and emerged as a nation in 1918 with their language and their Catholic faith intact. When communism ruled with an iron fist for four decades, the people continued to build their churches. Neither the Turks, nor foreign rulers, nor communists could compel the people of Poland to give up their faith. Faith was their armor against all calamities and enemies, shaping not only their interior world, but their outer world as well. Nowhere is this more evident than the Polish skyline, where innumerable church spires reach for the heavens. Nowhere is this more evident than in the landscape where every crossroad or open meadow is home to a little chapel, a wooden or iron cross, a statue of the Blessed Virgin Mary or one of Poland's much-loved saints. The spirit and history of Poland is written on its landscape.

It was in 966 AD that King Miesko I of Poland accepted Christianity. By 968 AD, a missionary bishopric (a bishop's cathedral for the propagation of the faith) was established in Poznań. It is difficult to ascertain the exact date and origin of when the crosses and figures of saints began to appear in the Polish landscape, but it is known that they arose around the time of the country's acceptance of Christianity.

One of the theories of origin dates the time to that of the Roman Empire and a cavalry officer by the name of Martin of Tours. Seeing a beggar with no coat, Martin of Tours cut his military cloak in half to give part to the beggar. The other half he wore over his shoulders as a "small cape" which in Latin is called a *capella*. Soon after his encounter with the beggar, Martin had a vision in which Christ was wearing the part of the coat he had given away, and Martin subsequently experienced a religious conversion. He first became a monk, then an abbot, then a bishop. Later canonized as St. Martin, Bishop of Tours, (331-400 AD), the patron saint of beggars, wine growers,

15th c. depiction of St. Martin dividing his mantle. Polytych from Dominican convent at the Church of St. Catherine in Wrocław.
Photo credit: Muzeum Narodowe w Wrocławiu (National Muzeum of Wrocław)

and innkeepers, he became one of the most popular saints of France whose feast day is celebrated on November 11. The small cape of St. Martin became a relic. The cell (the room in a monastery) where the small cape of St. Martin was preserved also came to be called a *capella*—a chapel or sanctuary for relics. With the passage of time, the word was transferred to mean any sanctuary or holy place containing relics. Later yet, the word came to mean any room serving to hold church vestments or a religious object. Even the exterior additions to churches began to be called a *capella*. In countries accepting Christianity, *capella*, or chapel, became a common term for any place of worship other than a church such as a room dedicated to worship in a private-dwelling house or palace or small building outside of a church that gave shelter to a religious object or figure. Later, at the

synod at Agde in Languedoc in AD 506, the church gave permission to the clergy to hold Mass and other religious services in such a building.

Among the countries that had accepted Christianity, the word *capella* became a universal name for any small building or roof that was used to cover a religious artifact. In Spain, the little chapels are called *capillas* or *capillitas*. In Italian, the word is *cappella*; in Slovak, *kaplnka*. According to Polish etymologist Jan Karłowicz, the term came to Poland through the Czechs and emerged as *kapla*, *kaple*, and eventually *kaplica* to mean chapel or little church. *Kapliczka*, a diminutive of the word *kaplica*, is an affectionate term that refers to something even smaller, so that "little chapel" became the general name given to forms of small sacred architecture such as the little church-like chapels, the religious figures on top of pedestals, and the crosses that dot the Polish landscape.

Polish ethnographer Zygmunt Gloger claims that legends tied to the first examples of small, sacred architecture in Poland along the roadside are associated with St. Adalbert (Św. Wojciech, 939-997). When the saint was traveling from Kraków to Gniezno, he stopped along the way to preach. In these places where he

Figure of St. Adalbert by woodcarver Michał Gier (1853-1929), Muzeum Etnograficznego im.Seweryna Udzieli w Krakowie (Ethnographic Museum in Kraków). Photo credit: Marcin Wąsik

taught the new religion, the locals erected a small shrine and supposedly the first was established in Modlnica, a mile outside Kraków.

By the 11th century, the first monks, the Benedictines, arrived in Poland followed by the Cistercians, the Dominicans, Franciscans, Augustinians, and Carmelites. All began teaching the new faith. The most powerful symbol of the new faith was the cross, Christ crucified, and it gradually began to replace the old pagan idols. Then over the ensuing centuries, historians, ethnographers, and the clergy of Poland as well as foreign travelers and pilgrims all noted the presence, importance, and abundance of the shrines and little chapels that could be found everywhere throughout Poland.

Many varied and interesting forms of chapels, crosses, and statues of religious saints have emerged in Poland throughout the centuries. They can be found in large city squares, entrances to towns, along dirt roads, streams, and rivers, deep off the beaten path and along major highways. Some are characteristic of the different regions of Poland and even within a region in Poland whose borders have changed and changed again there can be an unusual array of styles and motifs. The Spisz region in southern Poland favored chapels and crosses. In Śląsk there is a preponderance of stone crosses. In Warmia, adjacent to the Baltic, red brick dominated as the construction material. All are varied, imaginative, and inspirational.

Tadeusz Seweryn, one of Poland's first ethnographers on the subject of roadside shrines with his book *Kapliczki i Krzyże Przydrożne w Polsce* (*Roadside Shrines and Crosses of Poland*), identified these major categories of roadside shrines:

- crosses
- pillars, posts, or columns topped with a religious figure or a cross or with bas reliefs or niches for holy pictures or figures along its length
- small chapels
- small cupboard or shadow box, miniature chapel hung on trees or posts
- a niche within a private home

*Warsaw with cross in town square on Easter Monday,
Illustrated by Jan Piotr Norblin (1745-1830).*

CROSSES *BOŻE MĘKI*

> *Krzyż we wsi, Bóg we wsi.*
> A cross in the village, God in the village.
>
> —Polish proverb

The first symbol of the new faith was the cross. Small and large wooden crosses, stone crosses, forged crosses, and those mass produced as iron castings can be found as examples of the infinite combinations and varieties of small sacred architecture throughout Poland.

Besides being found within churches, large crosses were erected on roadsides throughout Poland. They came to be called *Boże Męki*, or God's Passion/Suffering. This custom of erecting large crosses along the roads of Poland became even more widespread during the 17th century after the Council of Trent (1545-1563). As a result of the Protestant Reformation led by Martin Luther and his attack on the beliefs and practices of the Roman Catholic Church, the 19th Ecumenical Council of the Roman Catholic Church laid down dogma clarifying nearly all the doctrines contested by the Protestants. This became known as the Counter Reformation. The Council called for the erecting and establishment of crosses and the renovation of existing ones. In 1621 a synodal decree demanded that parish priests ensure the sign of the cross was represented in all villages to demonstrate that Catholics had nothing whatsoever in common with heretics and pagans. Tall wooden crosses began appearing everywhere. Jakub Kazimierz Haur (1632 -1709) in his *Ekonomika Ziemiańska*, a tract published in Kraków in 1675, wrote that the Poles "establish crosses, that is, the Suffering Christ, along the roads, in the fields, near cities and hamlets." It was believed that only after erecting a cross did a village truly become Christian. A newly erected cross would be blessed by a priest when he visited the town or village for the first time.

Another ethnographer by the name of Zygmunt Gloger (1845-1910), in his four volume work titled *Encyklopedia Staropolska* (*The Encyclopedia of Old Poland*) published in 1900, entered a heading under *Boża Męka* (the Suffering Christ on the Cross) with this description: "This Christian symbol was erected by the pious at crossroads, at the site of battles and skirmishes ... wherever Christian blood has soaked into the soil ... the people erect the cross as thanksgiving for assistance in unbearable situations, in memory of an anniversary, to protect against communicable diseases."

In *Encyklopedia Kościelnej*, by Father Michał Nowodworski published in Warsaw in 1878, he states: "No other country to the present day

Roadside crosses in Wisiołek Luborszycki, Kraków region, 2007.

has as many crosses along the roadside, in the fields and country cemeteries as we do."

The oldest crosses were made of wood as it was a readily available raw material. The type of wood depended on the region. Oak was preferred as it was a hard wood and weathered well. Some crosses were made of resinous pine which was resistant to woodworms. While wooden crosses were the simplest to erect, they were, at the same time, the least durable. Thus they were purposely made massive in height so that when the wood deteriorated at the base, threatening to topple the structure, the cross was dug out, cut from the bottom and then reset in the same spot. This way the wooden crosses generally lasted about thirty to fifty years, and in some situations reached the age of one hundred. The site where a cross was erected is considered sacred, therefore when old crosses are removed, they are always replaced with new ones, even to this day, often made with a newer more durable material. If a cross were to be repaired, it was usually done on All Souls' Day (November 2) or at the end of April, in preparation for the May services. If an old cross was removed, it was usually burned on Holy Saturday or on the feast of St. Roch (August 16). There was a strong belief in folk culture that any person who tried to remove or destroy any cross would meet with grave misfortune, such as family diseases, fires, floods, hailstorms.

Latin Crosses

Ethnographer Tadeusz Seweryn identified many forms of crosses in Poland, but most emerge from the Latin (T) cross, the form on which Christians recognize that Christ was crucified. The Latin (T) and the Greek (+) forms of the cross are the oldest Christian forms, and at the same time they are the most basic so that infinite variations were made from them.

The most basic, plain form of the Latin cross is made of two pieces of wood, a vertical longer piece and a shorter horizontal piece. At the place where the two pieces of wood intersected there was sometimes a wooden or metal figure of the crucified Christ, called the corpus. A cross with a corpus on it is usually called a crucifix. The corpus or entire crucifix is sometimes protected from the elements by a strip of wood or sheet metal. The piece of wood or sheet metal could have some kind of open work or notched, serrated edge for a more decorative effect. This type of cross can be seen throughout all of Poland. Sometimes the local carpenter chiseled the date that the cross was

Cross in Gwizdów, District of Leżajsk, 2007,
with close-up of corpus protected by metal.

erected, the name of the person who funded the cross, and perhaps
some kind of inscription:

Który za nas cierpiał rany, Jezu Chryste, zmiłuj się nad nami
You who suffered wounds for us, Jesus Christ, have mercy on us

Niech nam Bóg błogosławi
Bless us O Lord

W krzyżu cierpienie, w krzyżu zbawienie
In the cross there is suffering, in the cross there is salvation

INRI on top of cross, Latin abbreviation for Jesus of Nazareth, King of the Jews, interior of roadside chapel, Kałuszynie.
Photo credit: Krystyna Bartosik

There are an infinite number of variations to be found to a simple Latin cross. Some have religious images all along the vertical beam of the cross such as angels and saints. Some carry the inscription INRI, the letters that Pontius Pilate had written over the head of Jesus Christ on the cross (*Isevs Nazarenvs Rex Ivdaeorvm*: Jesus of Nazareth, the King of the Jews). Some crosses also depict the *Arma Christi* ("Weapons of Christ")—the instruments and objects associated with the suffering of Christ. These might include any of the following: the abbreviation INRI, a crown of thorns, a post and lash for flogging, the veil of Veronica (a pious woman

Cross with instruments of torture called Arma Christi erected in 1932, Wilimy, Olztyn County. Photo credit: Marian Dąbkowski

Rooster on top of cross, Gwizdów, District of Leżajsk.

named Veronica stepped forward from the crowd and wiped the blood and sweat from the head of Jesus as he carried the cross through Jerusalem to His crucifixion), pliers and nails, a hammer, a shovel, a ladder, the moon and stars, or a rooster (referring to the betrayal of Christ by Judas).

On the landscape of Poland, especially in the Podlasie area in northeastern Poland, the Orthodox cross also has a lower, slanted bar. According to the Orthodox tradition Christ's feet are depicted as being nailed not at one point as seen on Catholic crosses but individually at the two sides of the footrest.

Wooden orthodox crosses, Berezyszcze, Podlasie region in northeast Poland, 2009. Wikimedia

There are also an infinite variety of decorative elements added to the horizontal ends of crosses such as carved knobs or trefoils. The trefoil is commonly seen on wooden crosses in the Podlasie and Kaszuby regions. Sometimes a small roof is seen as covering the figure of the crucified Christ or it can cover the entire top of the cross protecting the top portion of the cross and the arms from the elements. The roof sometimes had a backing made of slats of wood to protect the cross but also as a decorative element.

Cross with a small roof covering, Sól, Biłgoraj region, 2007.

A LEGEND FROM KURPIE REGION

The Puszcza Zielona, the Green Kurpie Region, in the northeast corner of Poland, was at one time a place of numerous crosses. On a church wall in Nowogród there was at one time a painting (lost during a remodeling in 1904) depicting Christ and a Kurp (a person from the Kurpie region) together carrying a cross to Golgotha. Adam Chętnik, an untiring scholar of the region, documented that the painting was connected to a popular legend:

The Lord Jesus left Pilate and began the road to death carrying His cross on the hill to Golgotha. He was tortured, beaten, dripping with blood and sweat and stumbled with the heavy load on the uneven road. The Jews who walked along were in no hurry to help. A Kurp passing by saw this and felt terrible sorrow for the person with the crown of thorns. He pushed his way through the throng and took the cross on his left shoulder which immediately eased the Lord Jesus. And Jesus looked over, smiled, blessed him and as the Kurp was leaving, said to him: For that, that you have a good heart, may you and your countrymen never be without wood – for your own needs and for crosses. And there grew the enormous forests of Puszcza Zielona, and the Kurps found themselves rich in wood and everyone who could, wherever they could, erected crosses.

Lithuanian Crosses

When Polish queen Jadwiga married Władysław Jagiełło, king of Lithuania, in 1386, the marriage united the Kingdom of Poland and the Grand Duchy of Lithuania, later known as the Polish Lithuanian Commonwealth, one of the most powerful unions of the time. One of the conditions of the marriage was that Jagiełło convert to Christianity and Christianize Lithuania, to which he agreed.

After the marriage, Jagiełło along with many other priests from Poland, went to Lithuania where Christ was yet unknown and where the ancient belief that trees served as residence or shelter for ancient gods was powerfully strong. Jagiełło began to promulgate the Christian faith among the people. The Lithuanians opposed the idea of one true God and argued against abandoning the customs and faith of their ancestors and their own deities, such as fires, snakes, and vipers, as well as the sacred groves in which these deities resided. Jagiełło

17th-century Lithuanian shrine, c. 1919-1939, Narodowe Archiwum Cyfrowe. National Digital Archives

Illustrations of Lithuanian crosses from the periodical "Wisła: Miesięcznik Geograficzno-Etnograficzny" 1903.

ordered the extinguishing of the sacred fires and the destruction of the altar on which sacrifices were made at the temple in Wilno (now Vilnius), the main city and capital of Lithuania, and zealously strove to establish the Christian faith so that it spread and strengthened. The people began to learn the main principles of the religion and gradually came to be baptized. Pious himself, Jagiełło founded a cathedral church in the city of Wilno. In 1386 Prince Jagiełło was baptized into the faith, and in 1387 Jagiełło established the Vilnius bishopric and construction began on the cathedral, which was dedicated to St. Stanislaus, the patron saint of Poland. This served to unite the two nations, Poland and Lithuania, not just by their respective monarchs but by faith. The two countries were as one from the late 1400s to the time of the partitions in 1795-1918 when it was divided by Russia, Prussia, and Austria.

Just as in Poland much earlier, the crosses in Lithuania were first erected as a method of converting the people from the old deities to the new faith. The transition from pagan beliefs to Christianity was eased by establishing Christian statues and crosses in the old sacred groves, by streams and on trees that were once revered. By the 1700s it is known that the Lithuanian countryside was filled with chapels and shrines of the saints as well as a tremendous abundance of crosses, which could be seen at the crossroads, at farms, in forests, in fields, and in cemeteries.

The area called Žemaitija (Żmudź, in Polish), also known as Samogitia, one of the five ethnographic regions of Lithu-

Procession in Żmudź, illustration by Stanisław Witkiewicz in 1878.

ania located in the northwest region of the country, was especially rich in wooden crosses, so much so that Wincenty Pol, writer, poet, and geographer of Poland called it "the sacred land of God." While there were many plain, simple crosses, there developed in that region a richly ornamental folk art form whose beauty and craftsmanship was exceptional. The special term for sculptors who made crosses was *dievdirbiai* (god makers). The tradition was passed from generation to generation.

During the partitions of Poland, Russia acquired the territory of Lithuania as well as the region called the Kingdom of Poland and both areas suffered after the January Uprising of 1863 when the people were trying to rid themselves of Russian domination. The Uprising failed and Mikhail Muravyov (1796-1866), the Russian governor-general, sent out an edict forbidding the erection of new crosses, repairing of old ones, and the enacting of any rituals and practices around the crosses and shrines throughout what was the Polish Lithuanian Commonwealth.

Even though the people secretly struggled to save the wooden crosses and shrines erected by their fathers and grandfathers, precious time was lost—over thirty-three years—until the edict was rescinded. The old carvers and highly ornamented construction gradually faded, and an artistic form was irretrievably lost. Polish periodicals, however, attest to the fact that there were still many crosses left in the Wilno (Vilnius) area in 1903 as well as concerns regarding their disappearance and the need to document them.

The greater concentration of crosses in Lithuania can be found in Samogitia, Aukštaitija, and Dzūkija. The Hill of Crosses, the *Kryžių Kalnas*, near Šiauliai, is one of the most unique places in the world. Crosses have been erected there intermittently since the 19th century with hundreds of thousands of crosses, many of them testimony to the extremely artistic work of folk masters.

Hill of Crosses, Šiauliai, northern Lithuania, 2018. Photo credit: Jan Filipiak.

The Caravaca Cross

When observing the numerous roadside crosses throughout Poland's landscape, one sometimes discovers a cross with two horizontal cross pieces. Typically, the upper cross beam is shorter than the lower one, but in Poland sometimes the two beams are the same length. This type of cross is called by many names but most frequently they are known as Caravaca crosses, *karawaka* in Polish. Their purpose was to protect the local people from epidemics and communicable diseases.

The first crosses with two horizontal cross arms as a means to

Caravaca cross, Sumiężne, Ostrów Mazowieka region, 2007.
Photo credit: Michał Zalewski.

protect against epidemics appeared in a Spanish town by the name Caravaca de la Cruz and it is from this Spanish town that the Polish word *karawaka* is derived. The city housed a relic—splinters of the Holy Cross in the shape of a cross with two horizontal cross beams. The relic was credited with miraculous powers protecting the town from pestilence, and soon crosses in that particular shape were erected throughout Spain. News of this spread quickly throughout all of Europe. It reached Poland by the second half of the 17th century through the efforts of the Jesuits, and Caravaca crosses began to be erected all over the country and were often called *krzyży hispanski*, the Spanish cross.

From the time of the Middle Ages, there were all kinds of epidemics, such as typhoid, typhus, and the bubonic plague, that swept through various regions of Europe, including Poland, decimating cities and entire villages by the thousands. In 1585, for instance, the city of Cieszyn suffered an epidemic of the black plague, killing three thousand people, accounting for two-thirds of the total number of its citizens. In some regions, the two-armed (and sometimes, three-armed) crosses were also called *krzyży choleryczny*, or cholera crosses, referring to the cholera epidemics that intermittently raged through Poland, often annihilating the entire population of towns. In the face of epidemic diseases, the population was virtually defenseless.

There was very little knowledge of what carried diseases at the time. Much of it was attributed to "bad air" and everyone turned to God with prayers to contain or reverse the epidemics, and also erected crosses, the strongest symbol of the Christian faith, to protect themselves. These crosses, chiefly made of wood, but in later years of metal, were usually erected at the beginning and end of the village or town boundary with the faith that they would prevent the entrance of "bad air" into the town and thus protect the inhabitants from contracting communicable diseases. The crosses were often inscribed with letters across the two upper and the horizontal beam that were an acronym of the prayer of St. Zachary and thus this type of cross was also called the cross of St. Zachary. It usually has seven little crosses and eighteen letters denoting the first word of the prayer/litany asking for protection against epidemics. The following are the first five of the twenty-five lines of the prayer, entreating the cross for protection. At every symbol of the cross the individual was to make the sign of the cross upon themselves:

*Letters on a Caravaca
cross from prayer book,
Warsaw 1894.*

1. + – *Krzyżu Chrystusów! Zachowaj mnie*
   Cross of Christ! Save me

2. Ż – *Żarliwość domu Twego niech mnie uwolni*
   Let the zeal of your house set me free

3. + – *Krzyż zwycięstwa, Krzyż panuje*
   Cross of Victory, the reigning Cross
   Krzyż rozkazuje, przez znak
   The Cross commands, by sign
   Krzyża Panie uwolnij mnie od
   Cross of the Lord, set me free from
   tego zaraźliwego powietrza
   this contagious air

4. D– *Daj Boże! Boże mój, uchylenie złego powietrza
   ode mnie i od miejsca tego*
   God grant! My God, lift the bad air away from
   me and from this place

5. J – *Ja w ręce Twoje Panie polecam ducha mojego,
   serce moje i ciało moje*
   I commend my spirit, my heart and my
   body into Your hands, Lord, etc.

Also often written on numerous crosses were the words "*Od pow-ietrza, głodu, ognia i wojna zachowaj nas Panie*" ("From air, hunger, fire and war, save us Lord"). Other inscriptions on these two-armed crosses included, "*Od naglej śmierć, zachowaj nas Panie*" ("From sudden death, protect us Oh Lord") inscribed along the whole length of the cross; and "*O Wielki Boże zachowaj nas od cholery*" ("Great God, protect us from cholera"). Help was also sought through prayers to other saints such as St. Roch or St. Rosalia, who according to folk tradition were given special powers to negate pestilential air. Ethnographer Zygmunt Gloger wrote: "During times of epidemics, the devout erected *karawaki* near villages and towns so that the epidemic would pass them by and they prayed on books with the same name."

Writing about the town of Suprasl in northeastern Poland, ethnographer Wojciech Załęski defines the erecting of the *karawaka* crosses as ancient pagan customs intermingling with the new faith. In that particular village, it was the responsibility of the entire village to participate in its erection, everyone having a predetermined role, and the entire project had to be finished by the first crowing of the rooster in the morning. It was believed that in order to be effective, the *karawaka* cross had to be erected between the hours of sunset and sunrise. Beginning at sunset, a plow was harnessed to a pair of white oxen and a furrow was made around the entire village creating a boundary, the magical safe circle, which the disease could not cross over, thereby protecting those within. At the same time, beginning at sunset and finishing at sunrise, the women were required to weave a linen cloth forty meters long and eighty centimeters wide called a *swojczyka*. During that time men would cut down an oak or an ash tree and hew it into a cross with two arms. Where the furrow made by the plow connected and enclosed the village in the safe circle, a hole was dug. Into this hole was placed an offering which was the cloth that was woven during the night, folded into forty layers. This offering was covered with a flat, pale stone, which in ancient times must have served as an altar. It was on this offering that the cross was mounted and, once in place, the cross completed the protective circle around the village rendering it safe from the pestilential air.

Besides being found at various crossroads, villages boundaries, and entrance gates to cities, the *karawaki* crosses were also placed near cemeteries where victims of the disease were buried. Sometimes they can be seen far from the town or village boundaries. This was often the site where epidemic victims had to be buried in mass graves.

Such a cross at a burial site was both a protective measure to keep the disease away, but also acted as a reminder of the loss of souls and the need to remember them in prayer.

Stone Crosses

In a whole class of crosses by themselves and most prevalent in Upper and Lower Silesia (Śląsk) in southwest Poland are *krzyże pokutne* (crosses of penance) or *krzyże pojednania* (crosses of reconciliation). These large rough stones carved into the shape of a cross can be seen in different parts of Poland, but they dominate this area because in its very earliest years, this area was colonized by many Germans to whom the erection of stone crosses was common practice. Many stone crosses are also found in Germany and what is now the Czech Republic and Slovakia. These rough, primitive stone crosses can be sighted almost anywhere—along the edge of a forest, ravine or gully; standing forcefully alone and seemingly abandoned in the middle of an empty field; or along an old road. Many stand lopsided in the earth, are damaged or falling into disrepair and in danger of disappearing altogether. Others have been recognized for the heritage that they represent and carefully maintained. Many have found a permanent home in local museums. Many of the stone crosses are without

Stone cross from the Middle Ages, Damianowice, Wrocław County.
Photo credit: Michał Zalewski

any identification whatsoever such as a date or signature to identify the sculptor, its purpose, or its origin. The oldest are believed to date back to the time of the Middle Ages. The most popular understanding about these stone crosses is that they are called crosses of penance, that is, carved by someone as part of the penance for committing a murder.

These earliest crosses were simple and made of local stone such as sandstone, gritstone, granite, basalt or more rarely, marble. By the 15th and 16th centuries, the stone crosses began to have engravings of crossbows, swords, stilettos, spears, and sickles. These have been interpreted as the instruments used to commit the murder. With the passage of time and as the common man began to learn his letters, real information began to appear on the crosses. On these later crosses information can be found about the time, place, the perpetrator, and the victim of the murder.

Metal Crosses

With the passage of time, the availability of iron, and the reality that wood eventually rots, metal crosses began to replace the wooden ones as they were longer lasting and less subject to decay over time due to the elements. There are chiefly two types of metal crosses: those forged by a village blacksmith or a guilded craftsman residing in a large city, or those mass produced as iron castings in factories and mills throughout Poland (but mostly in Śląsk, Silesia). Forged crosses have a longer history and at the same time are more interesting pieces of art.

Decorative elements on metal cross, Dąbrówka, Biłgoraj region.

The crosses forged by blacksmiths were either solid or with open work. The solid metal ones were made more decorative by adding shapes such as leaves, hearts, trefoils, or even another smaller cross at the top or ends of the side arms of the cross. Sometimes an important decorative element was the addition of rays emanating from the center of the cross. The most basic crosses would have four rays, one at each corner where the two arms of the cross met. Some had two rays or many more than that, often giving the effect of a monstrance. The forged crosses were placed at the top of steeples of churches, orthodox domes, gates to cemeteries, and on the roofs of roadside chapels. Smaller forged crucifixes were hung at the center of large crosses. Tall crosses made of iron forged in a blacksmith shop were also attached firmly to the ground, while the smaller ones were mounted into huge rocks or affixed to the top of stone columns and pillars.

LANTERNS OF THE DEAD, PILLARS, POSTS AND COLUMNS

"Lantern of the dead" was the architectural name given to independently erected towers near or in cemeteries and hospitals during the Middle Ages. Historians have determined that these first lanterns of the dead arose in conjunction with monastery cemeteries in the first half of the 12th century. The oldest known document referring to these buildings comes from the venerable Peter, Abbott of Cluny, during 1122-1156.

The towers were usually circular, made of stone, and topped with a cone-shaped roof with a cross at the peak. The upper portion of the cone-shaped towers had arches or open work. Some interiors had a small shelf. At the base of the towers was a door giving access to the interior where there was a pulley to raise the lamp or lantern to the top of the tower where the light could be visible by shining through the open arches. There are many interpretations about the purpose of the lighted lanterns at night. Since many of these lanterns were located near hospitals and cemeteries it is believed that they were a beacon to indicate the position of a hospital or cemetery at night. This is understandable when one considers that at dusk in medieval times, the city gates were closed and everyone locked their doors and shuttered their windows. People did not wander around the city during dark hours. But if you were sick, or believed to be dying, how to find the hospital? Others claim the lamps were placed to mark the position of the cemetery at night to warn the public that they were nearing a leprosarium, to ask for prayers for the sick, hopelessly ill, and dying, to ward off evil spirits and ensure peace for the souls of the departed.

Lantern of the dead from the Middle Ages, Kraków.

The lantern of the dead pictured here (*left*) initially stood at the hospital and cemetery of St. Walenty known as Kleparz. This was a part of Kraków along what is now Długa Street and still known as the Kleparz district. In the Middle Ages this hospital cared for lepers and those ill with the plague and smallpox. This tower was erected in the 14th century from blocks of sandstone. In 1871 it was transferred to the cemetery located near the church of Św. Mikołaja. It is a six-sided column topped with a coned roof with a small cross on top. The top part of the column is decorated with tracery. Unfortunately, the openings through which the light from the lanterns shown has been bricked over.

This lantern was captured in a painting by Teodor Baltazar Stachowicz (1800-1873) in 1845 (*below*). On the left side you can see the Church of the Holy Cross founded in 1390 by Queen Jadwiga and Władysław II Jagiełło for Benedictine monks of the Slavic rite called Glagolitic (Głagolica) who were brought from Prague. The monastery soon fell into decline and the church became a branch church for the collegiate

Świniary in southern Poland, erected in 1958, with a close-up of the inscription.

church of St. Florian in Kleparz. On the right is the church of St. Walenty, and behind that were the wooden buildings of the former hospital for lepers which later became a poorhouse. On the right side of the road, you can see the lantern of the dead which was transferred to the grounds of St. Nicholas Church (Kosciol Św. Mikołaja) in 1871.

As with many things, the lanterns of the dead lost their importance in the 14th century, but the particular style of the lanterns evolved into many forms and variations over the centuries particularly circular columns with figures of saints set on top. When the Protestant Reformation renounced the culture of saints and claimed that the one place to give worship to the Lord was a temple or church, the Roman Catholic Church said just the opposite: worship your holy saints or patrons and take your religious practices outside the walls of the church. The erection of religious figures on top of columns, pillars, and pedestals, and variations on all of these forms began to proliferate.

After the cross, ethnographers claim that the next evolution of the roadside shrines was a column or post with a cross or the figure of a saint on top. The oldest post-supported shrines are documented from the 15th century. They speculate that this particular method of erecting a shrine is based on the earlier lanterns of the dead that arose during the 12th, 13th, and 14th centuries. These structures arose chiefly in central and western France but also in northern Italy and Austria and reached into Czechoslovakia and Poland. The base contained reliefs and had numerous recesses or niches for sculptures, inscriptions, or paintings. By the 19th century this type of shrine with a pediment and smaller crosses on top had many variations and can still be seen throughout Poland. The three-tiered shrine with a crucifix pictured to the left was built in 1958 and reads: *O all you who pass this way, is there any sorrow like my sorrow.* (Lamentations 1, 12). The quotation from Lamentations is associated with the suffering of Christ during his Passion and often found incised directly on wooden crosses or on a column or pedestal containing a crucifix.

Other forms consist of pillars and pedestals topped with one of the many figures of the Blessed Mother, Patroness of Poland, or a saint who has been declared the patron of the village or town.

SMALL CHAPELS *KAPLICZKI DOMKOWE*

Kapliczki domkowe is literally translated as "little houses." This type of roadside shrine resembles a very small freestanding church almost always with a small altar inside.

The oldest brick or stone shrines preserved in the form of small chapels or churches containing small altars date from the 18th century. How these little churches came to be erected along the roads is not entirely known. Polish ethnographers surmise that their origin may be connected to the establishment of calvaries in Europe and Poland. Calvaries, also called passion sanctuaries, are places of great natural beauty that have been designed to imitate the hill of Jerusalem where Christ suffered and died. Within the landscape of these calvaries are many paths or avenues that lead to places of worship, usually small chapels and temples relating to the Passion of Jesus Christ and the life of the Virgin Mary. In Jerusalem, especially during Holy Week, services were held that followed the last week of the life of Christ culminating in the path of the cross—from the place of trial to Calvary, the place of crucifixion.

Small chapel built in 1890 in Szpitary in Kraków region, with the inset showing its interior. Pilgrimages stopped here on their way to Częstochowa.

Christian pilgrims returning to their home countries from the Holy Land frequently wanted to share their experience of the Passion of Christ and began establishing calvaries back home. The oldest European calvary was created in Spain in the 15th century and then in Germany and Italy. The time of the greatest establishment of calvaries in Europe, however, was during the Counter Reformation when the Catholic Church made tremendous efforts to negate the charges proclaimed by the Protestants and bring people back into the faith. In Poland, Kalwaria Zebrzydowska, nestled in the foothills of the Carpathian Mountains with its hills and valleys, was established in the early 1600s. The first ceremony depicting the Passion of Jesus Christ was celebrated in 1607. It became an extremely popular place of pilgrimage and pilgrims returning home from Kalwaria Zebrzydowska may have been inspired to create their own places of reflection and prayer and began building small chapels. The oldest known of these types of structures date back to these particular times and were endowed by individuals who could afford such an elaborate and costly edifice—priests, monasteries, and noblemen—people of substantial means and influence.

In the 18th and 19th centuries, with the emancipation of the peasants and the freedom to own land and the ability to gather some wealth, the shape and character of the small chapels erected along the roadside began to change. Rather than the elaborate Renaissance or Baroque chapels of the rich with domes and stained-glass buildings, the chapels began to be made of more humble materials. Some of the older chapels are made of wood simply because it was plentiful and at hand. Fieldstone plastered over with clay and then painted was another choice. Others were made of masonry or brick painted white or another eye-catching color.

The chapels are as varied and unique as the individuals or communities that were inspired to erect them. Sizes range from very small to very large, usually laid out in a square or rectangular floor plan, but circular and even octagonal ones can be encountered. Some are plain structures, others have decorated facades and peaks, often with a tower and ave-bell (also called an angelus bell, in Polish called a *sygnaturka*), a bell that was rung three times a day to remind the faithful to say the Angelus, in Polish "*Anioł Pański*" (*see page 139*).

Every chapel has a small altar where other holy figures and images are placed, indicating who the chapel is named for or devoted to. But the altars also serve as a place for hosting liturgy during various times of the year, especially in very small villages that didn't have a church of their own. Mass was said there by a visiting priest or the people gathered together to pray May or June devotions. Many chapels, as do other roadside shrines, have a gated fence surrounding the structure made of wooden or iron pickets to help designate that one is entering sacred space. Some are fenced in using live plantings such as shrubs or roses. Some have windows on the side walls, or maybe a front porch. In the history of the growth of Christianity throughout the land, a small chapel acted as the first church of a village until a larger, more substantial one, could be built.

In his epic poem *Pan Tadeusz: The Last Foray into Lithuania*, published in 1834, the fiercely patriotic Adam Mickiewicz left a lasting, inspiring written legacy of just what such a village gathering at a chapel looked like in the year 1812:

> Today, the Lithuanian people from all over the area
> has gathered around the chapel before sunrise …
> The mass began. The little sanctuary could not contain
> the entire throng; the folk kneeled on the grass,
> gazing at the door of the chapel and bared their heads.
> The white or yellow hair of the Lithuanian folk
> was gilded like a field of ripe grain;
> here and there a maiden's bright head,
> decked with fresh flowers or with peacock's feathers,
> and with ribbons flowing loose from her braided hair,
> blossomed among the men's heads like a cornflower
> or poppy amid the wheat.
> The kneeling, many-colored throng covered the plain,
> and at the sound of the bell, as though at a breath of wind,
> all heads bent down like ears of corn on a field …
>
> —*Pan Tadeusz*, Book XI

Small shrine on a tree in Zagródki, Biłgoraj County. Inset shows close-up of the shrine with the crucifix behind glass.

LITTLE CHAPELS HUNG ON TREE TRUNKS
KAPLICZKA SZAFKOWA / SKZYNKOWA / NADZREWNA

Writing in 1871, Polish ethnographer Oskar Kolberg wrote: "hanging on trees are altars, decorated in various ways with a paint brush or carving, some small some large, sometimes with a burning lamp before it."

Many ethnographers connect the placement of a religious icon on trees to the earliest days of Christianity when pagan thoughts and acts were still prevalent and not completely eradicated. Polish ethnographer Tadeusz Seweryn, pioneer in studying and recording Poland's crosses and shrines, claims that the custom of nailing small chapels to trees came to Poland during the early Middle Ages with the union of Polish queen Jadwiga to Władysław Jagiełło, king of

Lithuania in 1386. One of the conditions of the marriage was that Jagiełło convert to Christianity and Christianize Lithuania, to which he agreed. Lithuania was a country where the ancient traditions of trees as the residences or shelters of the ancient gods was powerful. In order to ease the way of acceptance to the Christian faith, the preachers of the new faith began nailing images of the new faith to the trees which were considered sacred among the pagans.

From the front it usually appears to be the facade of a little house or a church. It is usually composed of four pieces of wood—two pieces that make up the side walls, a back piece and a base. It is covered by a two-sided (gable) roof made of wood but can often be found made of tin. The front is left open so that a religious figure can be inserted inside or it is covered with a piece of glass to protect the image from the elements. These little shrines vary considerably. They range from a plain square box with a simple roof to more elaborate and decorative elements. The religious images inside also vary. It could be a sculpted figure carved from linden wood, or even a small wooden cross. It could be a painting of a religious figure on tin or glass, an oil painting, or even a woodcut. Sometimes the tree shrines only had a back side, on the order of a plaque, with or without a roof and with a cross or crucifix attached to the back. They can be seen along major highways, off the beaten path, and deep in forests. They are often found to be hung on pine, linden, oak, or poplar trees, trees that were once revered for their mystical powers.

These little shrines could also rest on top of a post driven into the ground or be attached to the side of the house. The custom of hanging small "private" box shrines on house walls, on trees in front of the farm, or on a post in one's own forest or meadow also grew. The variations are enormous, all dependent on the inner impulse and creative and spiritual visions of the people involved.

Sometimes these little box chapels were attached to the bottom end of a cross or at the center where horizontal and vertical beams meet or along the vertical beam. This is frequently seen in Małopolska (Little Poland). The wooden box consists of a back, sides, floor, and steeped roof with the front enclosed in glass or left open.

Blessed Virgin Mary in niche under the eve of a home in Huta Nowa, Tarnobrzeg region, 2010.

NICHE ON A HOME
KAPLICZKA WNĘKOWA

This type of shrine is considered to be the most private type of roadside shrine and is especially endearing. These are small recesses or niches built into the exterior wall of a private home near the gable, the place where roof lines meet. They are included in the list of wayside shrines because although they are built on a private space as opposed to the more public ones on the open roads and fields, they are often placed on the street side of the house for the edification of those passing by. The niche can be rectangular, or arched in a semi-circle, or more rarely, pointed in a triangle. The exterior area surrounding the niche may be decorated with colored glass, given some decorative molding, or enhanced with the initials of Jesus Christ and the Blessed Virgin Mary done in carving or plaster work. Tucked into this small space is a religious figure or holy picture. Sometimes the

Sorrowing Christ on the side of a home in Guczów, Zamość County, 2010.

Shrine on Marszałkowska Street, 2008.
Photo credit: Krystyna Bartosik

niche is covered with glass to protect the religious figure or holy picture from the elements. Within the house, this space is usually an attic and the inhabitants of the home have made it so that they have access to the niche through a removable wooden board that generally backs the niche. This gives them the ability to clean the glass periodically, change the flowers, or in the case of newer homes, the niche might be lit by an electrical light and the bulb may need replacement. The purpose of these shrines was to protect the home and its inhabitants against all misfortune.

The smallness of these shrines does not limit their impact, as attested to by this fragment of an interview with Andrzej Banak taken from the book *Moje Wojenne Dzieciństwo* (*My Wartime Childhood*). Andrzej, who was to enter second grade in September 1939, lived in a three-story building in Warsaw during the occupation of Poland during World War II:

> In many houses, statues of the Virgin Mary stood in the center
> of the yard, often with a halo made of small electric lights.
> In our building, the figurine stood in a small niche, between
> the windows of the owner of the building. One day a few of

the men known for their extraordinary piety built an altar under the holy image. A woman living in our building, famous for her rather quarrelsome ways, helped them arrange holy pictures and candles. And it was she who most often brought fresh flowers to this altar. Here every evening, after the curfew, a large group of tenants in the building and almost all the children gathered to pray aloud together for at least an hour. The Our Father, then the Hail Mary and I Believe in God ... Then there were litanies. Kyrie Eleison, Christe Eleison – have mercy on us. From all evil, save us, Lord. From hunger, fire and war, save us, Lord ... In the depths of my childish heart I took seriously these words spoken aloud and after such prayers I went to bed calmly for the night and the next day as well. It seemed to me that now we are safe and the war will end any day now.

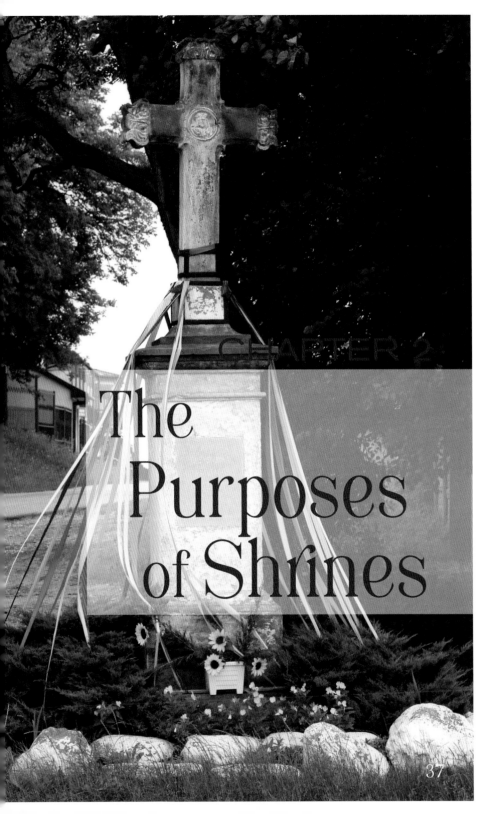

CHAPTER 2

The
Purposes
of Shrines

In many instances, the purpose or reasons for erecting many of the roadside shrines have been lost and forgotten over the years due to lack of documentation or the absence of individuals left alive to remember its original construction and intention. Many reasons were born within the secret recess of the heart and remained locked there forever. However, in oral histories and parish or town records, many complex reasons and motives are documented for the endowment of a chapel, cross, or figure of a religious saint either by an individual or through the initiative of an entire hamlet, village, or town. Though oftentimes all the reasons intermingled, they can be categorized as:

- protection against evil
- a prayer of thanksgiving or supplication
- a form of penance
- a memorial or remembrance

SHRINES AS PROTECTION AGAINST EVIL

The age of the ancient pagans was one of magical beliefs, specialized gods, and numerous rituals. With the acceptance of Christianity, the old beliefs and practices were hard to abandon. The pagans sought to protect their old beliefs while the propagators of the new faith tried to exchange the pagan idols with images and likenesses of the new faith. It is known that many ancient beliefs continued for many years, even centuries, after the advent of Christianity. Over time these ancient beliefs intertwined and intermingled with the new faith. Many of Poland's oldest shrines are found near trees that were once believed to have magical powers. The shrines were erected by already existing trees or trees were planted soon after erecting the shrine or chapel. Oak and linden trees were much favored. The linden tree, for instance, was considered especially sacred as protection against lightning and evil spirits. Sycamore and birch trees as well as pine and larch trees were also held in high esteem. There were sacred places such as special groves or a spring, the source of life-giving water that was also believed to have magical properties. Pagan shrines were placed at the feet of such places and various cult activities occurred there on a regular basis.

According to ancient beliefs, the outer boundaries of a village or a place where two roads met was considered to be an evil place where unfriendly spirits waited to pounce on an unsuspecting traveler. The chapels and crosses were holy objects and sacred spaces that could neutralize evil and were thus erected in what were considered possible areas of danger. Practically every hamlet, village, or town had such "dangerous" places. These were areas that belonged to no one, often lying beyond the reach of the sound of church bells—and according to beliefs of the time, likely places for the gathering of evil spirits, and meeting of witches and devils. Villagers believed that covens lurked there offering to sign contracts with the devil, as did condemned souls asking the living for redemption and rescue. Those who committed suicide or were condemned to death, as well as any unbaptized children, were all buried outside the boundaries of the village. It was believed that the soul of such an individual languished forever in this place of eternal unrest, sometimes changing into a ghost or vampire just waiting for someone to cross the boundary.

Besides burying the dead outside the boundaries of the village, various illnesses were often "transferred" there and sometimes people were executed in the location as well. The accumulation of evil in such places made people afraid to cross the "holy boundaries." In order to minimize the power of these dreadful forces, chapels and crosses were erected in these places. Situated on the outskirts of a village, they delineated the "safe circle"—the magical line where a person could feel safe.

Other dangerous dwelling places for condemned souls and demons were ponds, lakes, and rivers. Water spirits and water nymphs residing in these places waited for passersby in order to pull a victim into the water as new sacrifice or as an offering to the water gods. They often took on the shape of a will-o-the-wisp and became a shifting, elusive light seen over marshes or water. It was believed that the devil himself, full of hate and mischief, just hung around waiting for the unwary, unsuspecting traveler—someone running late for instance—and confused them into taking a wrong turn.

Chapels and shrines were also erected in places that were the site of tragic accidents: if someone accidentally drowned or died suddenly of unknown causes, was struck by lightning, or torn apart by wild animals, or perhaps crushed by an overturned wagon. The place

Bodies of villagers who died from cholera buried near shrine in Dębno, Zakopane region, 1931. Photo credit: Narodowe Muzeum Cyfrowe (National Digital Archive)

of death was often memorialized by erecting a chapel or cross, most often paid for by the family. The shrine served to keep the person's memory alive but also to protect the living against the return of the soul of the person surprised by death. The shrine prevented evil from settling down in a particular spot and perhaps causing further accidents. There is some similarity here with the Hispanic custom of *descansos*, associated with burials. In Hispanic tradition, before the time of hearses and motorized vehicles, caskets were taken to the cemetery on the shoulders of pallbearers. The men had to stop periodically to rest. The coffin was placed on the ground, the funeral procession prayed and then continued on. *Descansos* were places where those who carried the coffin from the church to the cemetery paused temporarily. These resting places were marked with flowers or two branches lashed together in the shape of a cross and planted in the ground. The tradition actively lives on today in the Hispanic southwest United States, and has also spread through much of the United States as well as Australia and Canada in the form of crosses erected at the site of traffic accidents where someone has died, where souls have left the body. Some people call it a cross-of-loss.

Another place where shrines were erected was at the site where a murder had occurred: for example, it could be two neighbors fighting over a boundary line or a betrayed lover and his woman. In the place of such an awful crime, the soul of the victim or the murderer would continue to hover and the shrine served to avert the evil.

The scariest places for the living were definitely those that were the site of mass burials and the sudden death of a great number of people. Plague and pestilence had troubled Europe throughout the centuries and Poland was no exception. Cholera, typhus, typhoid, and other epidemics raged through the countryside. They were as much a part of life as war, fire, and starvation. Sometimes the population of an entire village was wiped out. The dead were buried far from the village, away from where people resided. They were quickly and quietly buried in mass graves without the usual customs and traditions associated with one's final rest. When the disaster had passed and life began to return to its normal routine, the families of the deceased, or if they were also gone, the inhabitants of the village who survived, established a shrine or cross on the burial ground. The erection of a shrine accomplished many things simultaneously: it hopefully gave peace to the deceased, protected the survivors against their return to earth, and lastly, marked an important historical event and acted as a sad reminder of the disaster that had struck the village or town.

SHRINES AS A PRAYER OF THANKSGIVING OR SUPPLICATION

Within the Catholic Church there is an established ex-voto tradition. The term "ex-voto" comes from the Latin meaning "from a vow made." It is an offering to God, a saint, or other divinity as visible evidence of gratitude for some favor or blessing already received. This visible evidence would be a shrine of thanksgiving. Another form of the ex-voto tradition is to erect a shrine of supplication, that is, erection of a shrine in the hopes that prayers or a particular request or plea will be granted.

Very often the ex-voto, sometimes simply called a votive offering, can take on different forms such as a pilgrimage to a holy place, or an offer of money for a particular cause. It can be the subsidizing of a painting or a statue for within a church, but it can also include building an entire church or constructing a small chapel or statue on the side of the road. An example of a shrine of thanksgiving can be found

Chapel of St. Felicity,
Stalowa Wola, Subcarpathian region.
Photo credit: Stalówka.net

in southeast Poland on the river San, in the city of Stalowa Wola, where there is a small chapel dedicated to St. Felicity in remembrance of two connected events: the Galicia Massacre (*Rabacja Galicyjska*) and a family's personal experience with the event.

The years between 1831 and 1863 were difficult years for Poland. Partitioned and under the rule of Russia, Prussia, and Austria, the country was trying to regain its independence. Secret societies sprang up organizing attempts to obtain freedom. In 1846 there was to have been an insurrection in all three parts of Poland but it was crushed by the Russians and Prussians. The Austrian government did not send in troops but fueled the suspicions of the serfs by spreading the rumor that the insurrection was designed by the rich nobles of Poland to further enslave them. As a result, the peasants began attacking the manor houses of the rich, brutally murdering, raping, and pillaging primarily in the regions of Tarnów and Sanok. When the rabbles were nearing Tarnobrzeg in March of 1846, the very rich prince Lubomirski decided it was best to move to the other side of the River San and hopefully escape the hands of the horde. When he, his family, and servants found themselves at the edge of the frozen river, his groom advised that the frozen ice covering the river could crack and start floating downstream. One of the other groomsmen offered to determine the safety of the ice. He walked to the center of the river, the ice cracked and the man drowned. Lubomirski decided to stay with his property and risk his life and that of his family. Astonishingly, the rabble stopped short of their property. The princess Felicja Lubomirska, in gratefulness to the groomsman that the family did not drown in the river, erected a shrine near the road dedicated to her namesake St. Felicity. In the center of the interior on a plastered wall is painted a portrait of St. Felicity. Under the likeness is a plaque with this inscription: "The likeness of Felicity of Rome – widow, murdered in Rome R.P. 164, together with her seven sons was thrown into the river during the times of Caesar Anthony. Pray for the souls of the deceased. The Eucharist is the sacrament of life."

Some other examples of shrines of thanksgiving might be:

- On returning from a distant market, a man is caught in a blinding rainstorm and accidentally drives his horse and wagon off the banks of the road and into a rushing river. Above the raging waters he sees a vision of the Blessed Mother and drives the horses in that direction and finds purchase on the edge of the riverbank. He feels he most definitely would have drowned if not for the intervention of the Blessed Mother. In thankfulness for the saving of his life, he erects a chapel near the riverbank.

- A woman, childless for many years, becomes pregnant and safely delivers a child. She erects a chapel to the Blessed Virgin Mary in thanksgiving.

- An entire village erects a small chapel dedicated to St. Nicholas (often seen as patron saint of hungry children) for saving the village from starvation in the 1850s.

- A young man with little prospects working on the lands of a rich family falls in love with the daughter. He vows that he will erect a shrine to St. Joseph, patron saint of families, if the parents agree to their union. His prayer is answered and in gratitude he erects the shrine. Within this man's lifetime, knowing the reasons behind the erection of the statue, young girls come to the shrine with flowers to pray for a loving and caring husband.

Other personal reasons for establishing a shrine of thanksgiving might include: thankfulness for a successful harvest; the return to strength and health when all was hopeless; the satisfactory conclusion of an important task meaningful only to a particular individual.

This shrine of thanksgiving in Wola Żelichowska, Dąbrowa County, was funded by Poles in their native village after safely immigrating to America in steerage. The inscription reads: Pod twoją obrona uciekamy się Święta Boża Rodzicielko *(Under your protection we seek refuge, Mother of God).*

Shrines established as a form of supplication, in hopes that prayers will be answered, can be seen in the wooden two-armed *karawaka* crosses of the Kurpie region, with inscriptions along the length and arms of the cross asking for mercy against disasters: *Od naglej śmierć, zachowaj nas Panie* (From sudden death, save us Lord); or *O wielki Boże zachowaj nas od cholery* (O great Lord, save us from cholera).

When the establishment of shrines was forbidden in the Russian sector during the partitions of Poland, shrines were erected in secret and the prayerful patriotic inscriptions read "*Boże zbaw Polskę*" (Lord, save Poland), "*Boże wróć nam wolna Ojczyzna*" (Lord, return to us a free Fatherland), *Boże Błogosław Polska* (Lord, bless Poland).

***

These were the types of life events that gave rise to thoughts of building a shrine or erecting a cross. Sometimes it took an individual many years to accumulate the finances to buy the material, or to pay the artist if a carving or a special holy picture was required, but the people of Poland gave visible expressions of their thanks to God or their special patron saint in the form of wayside chapels and shrines.

Whatever the reasons, no matter the length of time it took to erect them, the votive offerings were and still are important spiritual transactions between a supplicant and God. The vow can be made openly and publicly by an entire community. The promise can be made privately while kneeling in church or while lying on a bunk in a concentration camp in the dark of night. In all situations, an ex-voto offering is always an act of faith.

SHRINES AS A FORM OF PENANCE

Besides being a form of thanksgiving or supplication, the ex-voto or votive offering tradition could also be seen as an act of contrition for personal or collective sins and the hope for purification, forgiveness, and reconciliation. It was a way of restoring a relationship with God, a way of making one's soul whole again and restoring order in the world.

The closest understanding that Polish ethnographers have about the crude stone crosses found in the regions of Upper and Lower Silesia called *krzyże pokutne*, or crosses of penance, is that they stand as witnesses to the laws of the Middle Ages that dealt with someone committing a murder. According to the laws of the time, someone who was convicted of murder was given certain conditions to fulfill as their punishment. These included paying for the food and beer of the judge and his helpers during the trial, paying for the expense of the funeral, ordering a certain number of masses for the deceased, and ordering a certain number of candles for the church. There was a community service component where the murderer was to pay for the baths of the poor and indigent at a bathhouse or provide a repast after the bath. One of the stipulations may have been to participate in a pilgrimage to some holy place and do so barefoot and bring back evidence of actually reaching the place. This was no small punishment as making a

Stone cross, Czerwieńczyce, Kłodzko County.
Photo credit: Michał Zalewski

pilgrimage in those days was a long and dangerous affair that sometimes led to the death of the pilgrim. Usually the last act that had to be fulfilled was the responsibility of carving and placing a certain size cross at the site of the murder. This had to be done in the presence of the widow and orphans of the deceased and a representative of the church or local official. The murderer had to carve the cross himself. The cross was erected in memory of the deceased, to prompt passersby to say a prayer for the deceased and also for the soul of the murderer. When the cross was completed, the murderer was also expected to pay a certain amount in damages to the widow and/or orphans. This concluded all the requirements and obligations imposed on the murderer by the church and state.

Because of their antiquity and lack of hard documented information and evidence, Polish historians and ethnographers have only been able to piece together bits and pieces of the true purpose of these earliest stone crosses. Because this form of punishment came to Poland through Germany, they feel the correct interpretation of the word to denote these crosses is *krzyże pojednania*, crosses of reconciliation—not penance or punishment, but reconciliation and so an act of forgiveness and agreement. That many of these crosses can be found near a church or on church property may simply indicate they were among some of the early tombstones not necessarily the site of a murder. They also raise the question of whether a common

The Robbers Chapel built in 1830 in Zawoj Policzna.
Photo credit: Google Street View.

man without the skills or implements of a stonemason could complete such an arduous task. Other researchers recognize the rough shape of the stone as being not of a cross but of a woman, an image of fertility and abundance still present in the minds of pagans back in the early days of Poland's acceptance of Christianity, a time that coincides with the erecting of the stone crosses. These issues about the earliest crosses are still being debated and explored.

Polish ethnographers have also documented the presence of *kapliczki zbojników*, that is, shrines supposedly built by robbers as penance for the expiation of their sins. These are likely to be found in the mountainous region of Poland where the highland robbers, the *zbojniki*, were involved in poaching, stealing, and killing. According to legends they were the Robin Hoods of Poland—robbing the rich to give to the poor. One of these is located in Dolina Kościeliska. Another is located in Zawoj Policzna. According to local legend, the founders of that chapel were robbers who erected it as a votive offering for expiation of their sins. Mass was said there on the Feast of St. John the Baptist (June 24), considered to be the patron saint of robbers.

SHRINES AS PLACES OF REMEMBRANCE

Very often roadside shrines were erected to commemorate religious events, or in memory of an important local or national event.

The history of Podhale, the region in southern Poland at the foothills of the Tatra mountains sometimes called the "Polish Highlands," is one of rebellions and uprisings against social and national oppression. One of the most famous uprisings in the Podhale region took place in the tiny village of Chochołow located on the Czarny Dunajec River. It is a tale worth telling:

> The year is 1846. Poland as a nation no longer exists. It has been wiped off the face of European maps since 1772. It is now controlled by Russia, Prussia, and Austria, with the latter annexing most of the land bordering the Tatra Mountains, including Chocohołow, and further north as far as Kraków. For years, Poland has been fighting the yoke of domination by foreign countries. There have been major uprisings and revolts led by such luminaries as Generals Kosciusko, Sowinski, and Chłopinski—only to fail again and again.
>
> On the night of February 23, 1846, at ten o'clock at night, using only a lantern to lead the way, thirty mountain men, armed only with scythes, pitchforks, and axes, successfully attacked and subdued the military at the Austro-Hungarian army post located on the outskirts of their village. The insurrectionists then made their way to the Austro-Hungarian border where they seized the customs house in order to secure money to keep themselves financially afloat. After stealing 601 florins and 40 rubles, for which these angry but honest men left a receipt, they destroyed the official seal of the Austrian Empress Teresa and the marker that defined the border as Austria and left one of their own which read, "This is now Poland."
>
> Returning to their village, the ringleaders and followers gathered together and in the best tradition of freedom

The shrine of remembrance in Chochołów. The inscription reads: "In memory of the Uprising of Chochołów. February 21, 1846."

fighters all over the world, they wrote and signed the Manifest of Chochołow: "People of Podhale ... join us ... we call upon your honor, as did our ancestors, to fight for Poland." The rebellion failed. The participants were jailed and the region subdued once more.

To commemorate the events of this night, the village of Chochołów erected a shrine of remembrance: that armed only with scythes and sickles the village took on the might of an entire empire in the fight for Poland's freedom. The figure of St. John Nepomucen was erected at the crossroads of Chochołów and Czarny Dunajec. Local folklore says that after the suppression of the rebellion, the people erected the figure with his back towards the neighboring village of Czarny Dunajec because they had refused to participate in the rebellion.

The Austrian sector was not the only region that saw Polish insurrectionists. The Russian sector also had numerous uprisings. Among them was the Uprising of 1863-64 (*Powstanie Styczniowe*), an insurrection mounted by Poles in Russia's Kingdom of Poland and Lithuania whose aim was the restoration of the Polish-Lithuanian Commonwealth. This story depicts how the erection of a cross or shrine could also be due to a very personal experience and memory. It is a story that has been handed down through the generations by a family in the town of Grzybów near Stąporków. The storyteller is Michał Telera, a young boy in the Russian sector of the partitions during the time of the Uprising:

> *Beyond the window the winter winds were howling, shaking the branches of the trees and knocking powdery snow to the ground. The blizzard seemed to be gathering strength with every gust. My sister and I blew on the small window in the kitchen in order to see anything outside but it was already getting dark and only the contours of the trees could be seen through the snow-filled clouds. In the room it was warm and pleasant, Tata [Daddy] was sitting on the bench smoking his pipe and Mama was darning our clothes. Brutus, our dog, lay near the stove warming his old bones. I enjoyed such moments when the family was together.*
>
> *In this idyllic mood with the wood crackling in the stove, there appeared a flickering light in the window. One minute it was there and in another it was gone, seeming as if it was getting closer to the house. Brutus lifted his head to listen, as if catching some foreign voices amidst the howling wind. He tore away and ran to the door with a sinister growl. "Someone's outside! I saw a light," I said to my parents. Tata turned up the light on the kerosene lamp, Mama stopped her work and the dog began barking loudly. At the same time we heard a thudding at the door and voices:*
>
> *"Open up! Good people, open up! We are Christians and we have a wounded man."*
>
> *Tata gave us the signal to hide behind the stove and unbolted the door. A gust of cold entered along with a man carrying a lantern and behind him another two carrying a wounded man under the arms. One could see they were*

frozen and tired. Their faces were red from the cold and over the collars of their sheepskin coats and fur hats lay a thick layer of snow. At their sides were short sabers, pistols in their belts and across their backs, double barrel guns.

"Please don't be afraid. We are from the insurgents. Our squad fought a battle not too far away. The Cossacks broke through our cavalry and cut us off from the main company. Our commander fell from his horse cut by a saber in the leg. We have been carrying him since yesterday. Blizen has been taken and in Odrowąz there are large forces of Cossacks and all the villages are occupied by dragoons and infantry. We'll rest for a while, cleanse the wound of our officer and move on to Końskie where there is a doctor and safe house. Have you seen military nearby?"

"I saw neither Russian, nor ours," Tata replied.

The men lay the wounded man on the floor. Tata lit another lamp. Blood gushed from the high boots of the officer and the wound, reaching from almost the waist right down to his knee was bound with a sash. I saw his terribly white face, covered with sweat, feverish. His eyes were half closed and he was breathing heavily. The soldiers took off their coats, sat down on the bench and ate the hot barszcz [a soup often made from beets, but sometimes from greens or fermented rye flour]. They were so tired they fell asleep sitting up. Then my parents began to care for the wounded man. Mama cut up the thick cloth pants in order to wash and dress the wound from which blood and pus began to ooze. It was impossible to remove the boots as any attempt caused tremendous pain. Tata washed around the wound and bound it with bandage made from our cloth shirts. In a weak voice the officer asked for water. He could barely lift his head to drink, then fell asleep.

We didn't sleep all night. The exhausted soldiers snored loudly and the wounded man was delirious. My parents attended the officer all night. The blizzard stopped. Tata released Brutus into the yard to raise the alarm if necessary of any approaching outsiders. The insurgents got up and after a brief prayer, drank a little warm milk. They wanted to leave right away to an estate near Końskie to provide their officer with care and safety. Tata absolutely forbade moving the injured man. The wound on the leg had congealed but every unnecessary movement caused it to open and bleed, which could cause his death. The soldiers didn't want to bring any troubles down on the family by the Russian soldiers. They promised to return quickly with a doctor and take the wounded officer to a safe place. Tata wasn't afraid, knowing that with this kind of weather and the fairly long distance from the skirmishes, no one was going to look for the insurgents here.

They moved out following the forest path through the high snow towards Końskie. My parents were convinced that that same day, perhaps by nightfall at the latest, a sled would arrive for the wounded man. But that's not what happened. Tata nervously paced around the room worrying if the soldiers were ambushed and after being tortured, would direct where their officer lay wounded.

The situation with the wounded man seemed to improve. He asked for something to eat but he was so weak that after a few spoonfuls he fell asleep. In order not to tire him out, he remained on the floor on his sheepskin coat. His personal needs and washing his wounds were taken care of by my parents, sending us out to the barn. Two more days passed. Of the soldiers, not a trace. The officer felt better, then worse. After going out to the barn and then coming back into the room again I could smell the unpleasant odor of rotting flesh. Staying in the house the entire time we hadn't noticed the offending odor. That night the wind picked up and it started to rain. It began to thaw. The wounded man began to fever and rave. Tata began covering the wounded leg with his old cloak.

In the morning, instructed by my parents, I took my sister Zosia and went beyond the river to our aunt's house in Grzybowa. There I told everything to my Ciocia [Aunt] Jadzia, who got really upset. She spoke of the stupidity on the part of her brother and exposing the children to danger. She even wanted to come back with us and talk Tata into reporting to the guards and say he was forced to care for the wounded man. We stayed the night as had been agreed upon earlier with my parents.

When we returned home I saw that the officer was no longer there. I was only 12 years old but I understood that they had either taken him or he had died. I asked Tata about it and he took me to the barn where the deceased lay on clean hay. He had a cloth tied under his jaw and his hands clasped together. Tata told me he died of gangrene of the leg.

The earth was still frozen. Even though the snow was melting it wasn't easy to dig in frozen earth. In the corner of the yard was a stack of hay covered with fir branches. We moved all the hay to another place and where that stack had stood, we dug a deep grave and there buried the body. Tata had gone through his pockets. He found a few silver monies, a silver pendant with a chain near his vest, a cross on his chest, a pistol and a short Russian saber. Tata cut off all the buttons on his jacket and vest as there was some kind of crest on them which could be later given to his family. All these little things were placed in a clay pot, except for the saber and pistol which were hidden among the rafters in the barn. The clay pot was hidden in or near the house. That I don't remember. We found no information on the deceased as to his name or where he came from. Tata was sorry that he never asked the soldiers who he was caring for.

A year passed after the death of the officer. No one came to ask after him. The insurrection failed in late spring of that same year (1864) that the officer died. It became more peaceful and less dangerous. Tata decided to place a cross over the burial site.

At one point in my life I left home and worked on an estate in Lithuania. I received a letter from Zosia, my sister, asking me to come home as soon as I could. She wrote that Tata was on his death bed. I returned but wasn't in time to say my final goodbyes. Mama was sick, my sister unmarried so I decided to stay in my family home. Zosia told me Tata's final words: "Remember the burial site of the insurgent. Have Michael make a new cross of oak."

Cross at Grzybów near Stąporków, Końskie County. Photo and story credit: Radosław Nowek

I did as my father requested and carved an oak cross. This time it was larger than the first. The years passed and when I had my own family and small children I recounted the history to them, that they always remember the hero that was buried in our yard.

The house and yard and farm buildings underwent changes over the years with new structures and old ones knocked down. During the demolition of the barn, a bundle fell down. It was the saber and pistol of the dead officer that Tata had hidden. I remembered then the clay pot with the small monies and buttons but I didn't know where to look for it. First Mama and then Zosia died. They may have known but I wasn't with Tata when he hid it.

The new century began ... Our oldest son went into the military, our daughter married and our youngest, Jan, stayed on the farm. I always reminded the children of taking care of the cross of the deceased officer. The cross was taller now so much so that the women in nearby homes began to come and sing and pray May devotions in honor of the mother of God. No one knew of the burial of the individual. In 1913, I changed out the cross with my son Jan once again.

From Jadwiga Nowak, granddaughter of Michał Telera:
"I never knew my grandfather ... but my father Jan stayed on at the farm. I recall how he once, returning from a get together with his unmarried male friends one evening, saw the shape of a woman kneeling at the cross and stroking the cross with her hands ...
He frequently told me of my grandfather and the insurgents and

Spirit of Place

reminded me to keep the memory of the grave alive. He told me frequently of his vision of the kneeling woman. He thought that the family may have somehow discovered the remains of their ancestor. But he always saw the figure from a distance and when he approached there was no one there ... I never forget about maintaining the cross. Today it is cared for by my granddaughter's husband. He single-handedly carved the arm of the cross and replaced it."

* * *

During the partitions of Poland, the crosses and shrines became a fight against Germanization and Russification policies, then later against Nazi occupation during World War II, and then again against the totalitarianism of communism in the Polish People's Republic after World War II. The little wayside chapels and shrines were so ingrained in the national consciousness, so powerful, that the governments occupying Poland forbade their erection and refurbishment and even actively destroyed them. Such was the response after the January Uprising of 1863-1864 (*Powstanie Styczniowe*). Mikhail Muravyov (1796-1866), the Russian governor-general, not only subdued the rebellion, but unleashed a reign of terror, sending thousands of Poles into exile in Siberia. Believing that the responsibility for the rebellion lay within the church and clergy, he not only forbade the erection of new crosses and shrines, but also the refurbishing or renewal of them, as well as gathering at the shrines for prayers and any customs that took place with them throughout the year. The edict was not rescinded until 1896.

Shrine in Krzyżanowice, Radom County. The inscription, worn down through the years, reads: "In memory of achieving independence of our Fatherland."

The situation was similar under Otto von Bismarck and his Kulturkampf in the Prussian section of partitioned Poland. He tried to limit the influence of the Catholic Church, tried to abolish the Polish language, and mandated the German language be taught in schools. The Austrians, on the other hand, were more amenable and did not forbid erection of shrines or chapels nor did they destroy existing ones which accounts for the numerous shrines still extant in the Carpathian, eastern and southern portion of Poland today.

Despite the bloody suppression of national insurrections, exiles to Siberia, and increasing Russification and Germanization policies, the spirit of the Poles remained alive. They refused to give up their dreams of regaining national independence. The achievement of it came on November 11, 1918. After 123 years of partitioning by Russia, Prussia, and Austria, Poland was free again and shrines of thanksgiving which commemorated the event can be seen throughout the country.

Poland did not enjoy its independence for very long though. World War II and the occupation of Poland by Germany brought catastrophe and death to Poland unlike any other war. The history of one such memorial shrine tells this story:

> "This shrine stands near my family home. It was established right after the first World War in 1918 in memory of the soldiers who died in the battles with Germans in 1915 in nearby Leszno and Zaborowo. During World War II there were also some heavy battles here, specifically in September of 1939 in the protection of Warsaw during the invasion of Poland and again in August of 1944 during the Warsaw Uprising. When the Uprising was dying out, the soldiers of AK (Armia Krajowa, the resistance army) escaped to the nearby Puszczy Kampinoska (Kampinos

Memorial to soldiers of World War I and II, Leszno near Zaborowo, northwest of Warsaw, 2003.

Forest). My grandfather, who was helping the partisans, was found out and the Germans shot him. He was 46 years old. The local people hurriedly buried the dead under this local shrine. Later, the bodies were transferred to the local cemetery. The people in this region suffered terribly with the Germans burning the villages because it was close to Warsaw. To this day, the people care about this shrine and care for it."

—Krystyna Bartosik story, 2003

No one remembers exactly when the large wooden cross was erected in the forested region of Gielnia in southeast Poland. It was already there when Germany occupied Poland and World War II began. Given the order to evacuate all the villages in the region, the Germans were making sure everyone left their homes. The cross became the collection point of all the men, women, and children of the village. As they stood there with their bundles under what must have been the protection of the cross, a minor miracle unfolded. One of the women of the village, German by descent but living in Poland all her life, stepped forward and begged the officers to spare the village. It was considered a miracle that the inhabitants were spared. The people of Gielnia continued to live their quiet existence at the edge of a vast forest and to care for the cross that was the sight of their salvation.

Another shrine also recalls the events of occupied Poland during World War II but it's one that remembers the tremendous cost to civilians at the hands of the German occupiers. There was hardly a town in the region

Cross at Gielnia, Stalowa Wola County.

Memorial at Goliszowiec, Stalowa Wola County, with a close-up of one of the two plaques that give the names and ages of the forty-one people who were executed there on September 30, 1942.

of Lasy Janowskie, a massive forest in southeastern Poland, that was left in peace during the occupation. The forest hid members of the underground resistance army and the surrounding villages were suspect in helping to feed and clothe them and provide information on the whereabouts of German soldiers. In retaliation, the Germans held the "pacification," i.e., the execution, of entire villages. One of them was Goliszowiec. Forty-one people, ranging in age from 2 to 78, were executed and buried in a mass grave where they remain to this day. The memorial stands on the burial ground which is delineated by a fence.

During World War II and the occupation of Poland, the Germans did not just suppress the Catholic Church and the building of new shrines and crosses but actively destroyed them. In the area of Poland

A cross brought down by the Germans.

Figures of saints removed by German soldiers.

Statue of Christ removed by the Germans.

(Photo credits: Poland in Photographs 1939-1944. Collections of the New York Public Library. Astor, Lenox and Tilden Foundation)

incorporated into the Third Reich during the occupation of Poland, the German authorities ruined all the roadside crosses in Sieradz itself and the surrounding region on the occasion of Hitler's birthday on April 20, 1941. In her "Chronicle of the Occupation of the Convent of the Ursulines in Sieradz 1939-1945" (*Kronika Okupacyjna Klasztoru Sióstr Urszulanek w Sieradzu*), Sister Paulina Jaskulanka wrote: "

> *Early this morning Sister Emma Dropiewska returning from night shift at the hospital noticed that the cross in front of our church was knocked down and leaning on the fence near the bell tower! She ran into the back yard knowing that the sisters*

Spirit of Place

working in the gardens are up early, even on Sunday and told Sister Pankracja Łukasiak what happened. Immediately, with Sisters Michała Krakowiak and Sisters Emmanuela and Walercia Marsz, they ran to the front of the church and with much difficulty lifted the heavy cross and brought it inside the convent to the cloister."

Another entry for that day by Sister Ludwika Miedźwiecka at the convent states:

On this night the crosses and roadside shrines in town, in the surrounding countryside and in the cemeteries, the crosses were broken, the monuments shot at — in this way the Hitlerites celebrated the birthday of the Führer, the sacrilegious acts offered as a gift.

∗ ∗ ∗

In the earliest years of their appearance, the crosses and religious figures were a symbol of the faith of the people of Poland. Then the erection of crosses and shrines in Poland eventually became a form of resistance against Protestantism. Then they came to be a form of opposition against the governments that tried to crush the Polish spirit and destroy the country as a nation. As a religious object placed in a public space, they symbolized the courage and resistance of a community, of the country itself, to the powers trying to control them. Thus by the 18th century, the presence of little chapels and shrines had risen to the rank of a national symbol.

The policies of foreign invaders to destroy the crosses and shrines of Poland and deny the people of Poland even the right to build shrines on their own property without incurring harsh fines and penalties had the reverse effect from the invader's intention: instead of dividing the Polish people, it created a tighter unity among them. Individuals and communities secretly took down their shrines and hid them in order to preserve them. In defiance of any rules, the people of Poland erected their shrines overnight, in secret, in out of the way places, and deep into the forests away from prying eyes.

Left: *Cross dedicated May 19, 1990, in Kraków to the Polish soldiers murdered by the Russians at Katyń in 1940. It is located at the foot of Wawel Hill near the Church of St. Giles (Św. Idzi).*

Chapel of St. Joseph the Worker, built in 1901. Photo credit: Wikipedia

At the National Park in Ojców stands a chapel dedicated to St. Joseph the Worker. Legend states that the unusual location was due to the Russian edict forbidding the building of chapels and shrines on the property grounds—so they had built the chapel on water. The Polish spirit could not be broken.

CHAPTER 3

Religious Figures

There are great regional diversity and preferences throughout all of Poland regarding religious figures that are found in the chapels and statues. The great majority of religious images both in picture and figure form, however, represent Jesus Christ—Christ crucified, Christ bearing the cross or stumbling under the weight of the cross, Christ in his mother's arms (the Pieta), Sacred Heart of Jesus, Jesus of Nazareth, Infant Jesus of Prague, or the Sad Christ, also known as the Man of Sorrows or the Sorrowing Christ.

THE SORROWING CHRIST
CHRYSTUS FRASOBLIWY

The image of a man sitting with his head resting on the palm of his hand deep in thought, displaying tiredness or resignation or suffering, is known in the art of many countries as the Sorrowing Christ or the Man of Sorrows. This religious figure is one of the most well-loved religious icons in Poland, filling thousands of roadside shrines throughout the countryside. The Sorrowing Christ (*Chrystus Frasobliwy*) has regional names as well. In Kraków it is called *Święta Turbacyja*; in Śląsk, *Starośliwy*; in Kashuby, *Płacibóg*; in Podhale and Łowicz, *Miłosierdzie*.

Jesus of Nazareth, also called Christ before Pilate, by unknown 19th-c. artist.
Photo credit: Jaciek Kubiena. Courtesy of Muzeum Etnograficznego im. Seweryna Udzieli w Krakowie (Ethnographic Museum in Kraków)

The most common likeness that is widespread throughout Poland depicts Christ sitting on a block of stone or wood, crowned with thorns, stripped of clothes except for a loin cloth, his head resting on the palm of his right hand supported by his elbow on his right knee in the universal gesture of weariness and deep sadness. He appears tragically alone and beaten down. This image of Jesus Christ was, and continues to be, an image that generates an emotional response in everyday individuals who could relate to the feeling of being downtrodden and in despair. It has only gained in popularity over the centuries. According to the apocryphal legends of the Church, the Sorrowing Christ illustrates one of the events of the Passion of Christ in a scene called "Waiting for the Crucifixion," which depicts the Savior sitting on the hill of Calvary, crowned with thorns, naked except for a cloth over his loins with his head resting on the palm of his right hand. The oldest wooden roadside shrine with a likeness of the Sorrowing Christ was located in Anielów and was dated May 1, 1650.

Oldest known shrine with Sorrowing Christ from village of Anielów. Photo courtesy of Muzeum Etnograficznego im.Seweryna Udzieli w Krakowie (Ethnographic Museum Kraków)

Based on archival material, historians and ethnographers date the appearance of the image of the Sorrowing Christ in Poland to the late Gothic period at the end of the 15th century and beginning of the 16th century. The image already existed as a religious icon in Germany and France at the end of the 15th century and was believed to be brought to Poland primarily by the Franciscan, Dominican, and Bernardine monastic orders. The Bernardine order, for instance, dictates that its members reflect on the life and suffering of Christ. The most well-known late gothic sculpture of the Sorrowing Christ is found in the Church of the Holy Spirit (Św. Ducha) in Sandomierz.

Spirit of Place

Various versions of the Sorrowing Christ existed in religious icons over the centuries. In the Baroque period (1555-1750) the likeness of the Suffering Christ is crowned with thorns wearing a king's mantle. The mantle is pinned at the chest and covers one of his shoulders; the torso and rest of his body is naked with the exception of his hips, which are covered with a loin cloth. In this version, Christ also holds a reed-scepter. This form can be seen throuhout Poland but is most characteristic in Upper Silesia and the mountainous Carpathian region known as Podhale. In the Kurpie region and down through to the eastern Rzeszów areas, one can see the Sorrowing Christ wearing a long robe.

Other forms of the Sorrowing Christ include: Christ sitting on a block of stone or wood, crowned with thorns, naked except for a cloth over his loins, his hands tied together resting on his knees; Christ resting on a stone block or a wooden cross with the instruments of his suffering lying nearby, and surrounding the Savior are three executioners drilling holes in the arms of the cross or there are other spectators present such as the Sorrowful Mary. In another form, the Sorrowing Christ sits on a cross on the ground or it lies at his feet, sometimes the figure wears a soldier's uniform. This version of the Sorrowing Christ was sometimes used in erecting wayside shrines to commemorate those who took part in the Uprising of 1863.

Initially, the sculpting of the Sorrowing Christ figure was the work of skilled artisans, commissioned by wealthy nobles or the church hierarchy for churches and monasteries. It was, however, in folk art that the Sorrowing Christ gained tremendous strength and popularity. The image captured the minds and heart of the common people of Poland—people who toiled the land, struggled each day to eke out an existence and who often felt alone against the world. In their eyes the image not only personified a God reflecting on the evil of the world, worried and troubled by sinners, but was a symbol of their own everyday troubles, an expression of their oppression, of being downtrodden and put upon as serfs.

Left: *Sorrowing Christ with long robe, Museum at Stalowa Wola, Subcarpathian Rzeszów region.*

MARIAN SHRINES

The Blessed Virgin Mary has soothed the troubled hearts of the people of Poland throughout the centuries and is deeply tied to the life of the Polish people in prayer, in song, and in the innumerable roadside shrines that are dedicated to her honor. The Blessed Virgin Mary is one of the most popular subjects in roadside shrines which testifies to the unremitting cult of Mary that presides in Poland.

The most well-known versions include the Virgin Mary and the crucified Christ (Pieta), Blessed Mother of the Most Holy Rosary, Our Lady of the Immaculate Conception, Our Lady of the Miraculous Medal, Our Lady of Fatima, Our Lady of Lourdes, Our Lady of Perpetual Help, Immaculate Heart of Mary, and numerous variations on Mother and Child.

There are also numerous Marian sanctuaries throughout Poland—places of miraculous apparitions and sites of pilgrimages devoted to the Blessed Virgin Mary. Wayside chapels and shrines were erected in specific regions to honor a particular local Marian image such as:

> *Matko Boska Skępska* (Our Lady of Skępe) can be found in Kujawy, Kurpie, and northern Mazowsze. Mary is usually depicted without the Christ Child, hands folded together, most frequently with a crescent moon under her feet (but not always).
>
> *Matka Boska Kodeńska* (Our Lady of Kodeń), Queen of Podlasie, located in Kodeń in eastern Poland
>
> *Matka Boska Ostrobramska* (Our Lady of Ostra Brama; Our Lady of the Gate of Dawn) located in Wilno (now Vilnius). Mary is depicted with her arms crossed over her breasts.

But the most famous and well-known image, the most cherished image, of the Blessed Virgin in Poland and found in countless chapels and shrines, is Our Lady of Częstochowa. The image of Our Lady of Częstochowa, known throughout the world as the Black Madonna, depicts a dark-complexioned Blessed Virgin Mary holding the Infant Jesus. The early origins of the painting is unknown for certain but according to tradition the original was painted in the Holy Land and taken to Constantinople by St. Helena of the Cross in the 4th century.

Our Lady of Skępe by unknown 19th-c. artist.
Photo credit: Jaciek Kubiena. Courtesy of Muzeum Etnograficznego im. Seweryna
Udzieli w Krakowie (Ethnographic Museum in Kraków)

Shrine to Our Lady of Częstochowa, Łysaków.

Her son, the emperor Constantine, erected a church in its honor and the painting remained there for five hundred years. After changing hands a few times, the portrait came into the possession of a Polish prince named Ladislaus (Władysław) in the 15th century. Invading Tartars besieged his castle and an enemy's arrow pierced the image in the throat inflicting a scar, which remains on the painting to this day.

Legend tells us that Ladislaus, determined to save the painting from future attacks, decided to move it to his birthplace, Opole. While moving the painting to his own town he stayed at a small town called Częstochowa where he placed the painting in a small church. In the morning, when he tried to leave, the horses pulling the cart with the painting refused to move. No matter what they tried, the horses would not budge. Ladislaus understood this to be a sign from heaven that the image should stay in Częstochowa. He replaced the painting in the Church of the Assumption with the painting of the Black Madonna on August 26, 1382, a day still observed as the feast day of Our Lady of Częstochowa. Ladislaus then assigned the church with the painting to the care of the Pauline Fathers at the Monastery of Jasna Góra. In 1430, the Pauline monastery was plundered by the Hussites who tried to carry off the painting but were also unable to do so. One of the plunderers drew his sword and slashed the image twice, causing two deep gashes. Miraculously, the image remained with the Pauline order.

In later years, during the time of the "Deluge" in Polish history (*potop szwedzki*), Swedish armies invaded the Polish–Lithuanian Commonwealth and the country was almost totally conquered by the foreign invaders. The king was in exile. It was thought that all was lost but one of the places that still resisted the Swedes was the holy monastery at Jasna Góra—the most sacred place in Poland containing the icon of the Black Madonna, Our Lady of Częstochowa. The news that all was not lost galvanized the country into greater resistance against the Swedes. A new army was formed in support of the exiled king John II Casimir who managed to reach Lwów, one of only two major cities of the Commonwealth not seized by any of Poland's enemies (Gdansk was the other), and marshal his forces.

On April 1, 1656, during a Mass in the Latin Cathedral (also known as Archcathedral Basilica of the Assumption of the Blessed Virgin Mary) in Lwów (today Lviv in Ukraine), John II Casimir entrusted the Commonwealth to the protection of Our Lady of Częstochowa, whom he announced as The Queen of the Polish Crown and of his countries. In a painting by Jan Matejko in 1893, the royal vow is depicted by a scarlet banner with a white eagle. Dressed in black, the king kneels before an altar accompanied by his queen, Maria Ludwika. Witnessing the event was Stefan Czarniecki, the master of warfare, holding a saber, kneeling at the foot of the stairs. This is an excerpt from his oath, known as The Lwów Oath (*Śluby Lwowskie*):

> *I choose you today as my Patroness and Queen.*
>
> *Great Mother of God, Most Holy Virgin. I, Jan Kazimierz, for the love of Your Son, King of kings and my Lord and Your merciful King, having fallen at Your Most Holy feet. I choose You today as my Patroness and Queen of my countries. I place both myself and my Kingdom of Poland, the Duchy of Lithuania, Ruthenia, Prussia, Mazovia, Samogitia, Livonia,*

Painting of the Lwów Oath of Casimir II in 1656 by Jan Matejko (1893) currently located at the National Museum in Wrocław. Courtesy of Wikipedia.

Smolensk, Czernichów and the army of both nations and all my peoples, to your special protection and defense, I humbly offer my sorrowful Kingdom against the enemies of the Roman Church.

Because of your extraordinary favors I am compelled, together with my people, to a new and passionate desire to dedicate ourselves to Your service, I vow, therefore, that I, as well as senators and my people ... will worship you in all the lands of my Kingdom and I will spread my devotion to You....

The Commonwealth forces finally drove back the Swedes in 1657 and then the Russians in 1661. King Michała Korybuta Wiśniowski vowed the same at Jasna Góra on December 7, 1669. He begged the mother of God "Support me and this Kingdom—not mine, but yours, in all troubles." In later years, when King Jan Sobieski III (reigned 1674-1696) began his fight against the Turks at Vienna in 1693, he also entrusted his kingdom to the protection of Our Lady of Częstochowa and saved Europe from Muslim domination. With Mary's name on their lips and her likeness painted on their armor and flying high on their banners, the kings and knights of Poland fought against the Tartars, the Turks, the Swedes, and all foreign invaders.

During the 123 years of partitions of Poland, when Poland as a country was erased from the maps of Europe, Our Lady of Częstochowa at Jasna Góra became a symbol of identity and unity. Poles in all three partitions regarded Jasna Góra as a symbol of their national sovereignty and in spite of the political situation, Poland remained alive in the nation's collective consciousness. "Our Lady" was the sovereign of the country, the Queen of Poland and the Grand Duchess of Lithuania and nothing could change that. During the Uprising of 1863-1864 (also known as the January Uprising), an insurrection principally in the Russian partition to restore the Polish–Lithuanian Commonwealth, every insurrectionist wore a small scapular with the picture of Our Lady as a reminder that through her intercession, Mary was the nation's hope for regaining its freedom and becoming independent again. The thoughts and hopes and dreams of becoming an independent nation were so eloquently spoken by poet Zygmunt Krasiński:

Wskrześ nas, O pani, przed świata obliczem.
Raise us, Our Lady, from the dead in front of the world.

After the insurrectionists were defeated, the Russian authorities did their utmost to ban any propagation of the Marian cult. In police reports, Mary was described as "the most dangerous enemy" and the Russians essentially waged war against her. They closed the seminary at Jasna Góra as well as the printing press run by the Pauline Fathers. Pictures of Mary, Queen of Poland, with the white eagle were confiscated when found in private homes as were prayer books containing prayers dedicated to her. The Russians refused passports enabling

Blue and white flag on Marian shrine, Duszniki, Poznań region. Photo credit: *Region szamotulski-kulturalno-historyczny.*

pilgrims to cross district borders within the kingdom to visit Jasna Góra and tried to obstruct and limit the routes so that pilgrims carrying statues had to wander through fields and forests. In spite of numerous difficulties placed in their way, pilgrims still came to Jasna Góra from all districts. The pilgrimages never stopped, and in fact even rose in numbers.

In the Prussian sector, with its repressive *Kulturkamf,* when the Polish language was removed from all public and administrative buildings and schools, convents were closed, and severe restrictions were placed on churches, more and more religious activities centered around a local shrine or chapel on private property, a place where the police could not interfere. The shrines, with their dedications in Polish, and where prayers could be said and songs sung in Polish, essentially became a protest and revolt against the cessation of prayers and services in Polish churches. Through national triumphs and tragedies, amidst the demands of enemies and hostile governments, the image of Our Lady of Częstochowa has held the people of Poland steadfast in their common goal and they have emerged whole.

The icon of the Black Madonna, Our Lady of Częstochowa, is without a doubt the most important Marian shrine in Poland. The Pauline Fathers have devoutly protected the image for close to six hundred years at the Monastery at Jasna Góra in Częstochowa and it is visited by millions of pilgrims every year. *"Pod twoja obrona uc-iekamy, święta Boża Rodziecielko"* ("To your protection we flee, oh holy Mother of God") has been the byword of Poles for over six centuries and continues unwavering to this very day. To watch pilgrims approach the icon at Częstochowa humbly on their knees, to count the vast numbers of roadside shrines, chapels, sanctuaries and churches dedicated to her is to just begin to understand the depth to which the image is revered. The Marian flag, a bicolor flag of white over blue (the colors associated with Mary), can be seen at churches and roadside shrines dedicated to her. The feast day of Our Lady of Częstochowa, August 26th, is celebrated with tremendous reverence both in Poland and in Polish diaspora communities throughout the world.

SHRINES HONORING SAINTS

From the beginning of Christianity, the church has venerated persons who led lives of holiness or who suffered and died for the cause of God: the martyrs who died in persecutions, the virgins, the prophets, the apostles, and all who are remembered for their good works. Catholic feast days first arose from the very early Christian custom of the annual commemoration of martyrs on the dates of their deaths. During their persecutions in the Roman Empire, the names and dates of individuals who were executed were carefully recorded. In the third century the bishops began also listing names of persons who did not reach the point of execution but died a natural death after having experienced persecution. These were holy people later canonized as saints.

The practice of adopting patron saints harks back to the time of the building of the first public churches in the Roman Empire, most of which were built over the graves of martyrs. The churches were then given the name of the martyr and the martyr was expected to act as an intercessor for the people who worshipped there. Christians then began to dedicate churches to other holy men and women who were not martyrs but saints. The cult of relics evolved during the Middle Ages and the building of a new church, more specifically the altar, then required the relics of a saint. To this day a relic of a saint is placed inside the altar of each Polish church. The church would be named after that particular saint. Every church adopts its own particular patron becoming St. Stanislaus Church or St. John Kanty or St. Adalbert.

In Poland's long and venerable history since the acceptance of Christianity in 966 AD, and with a long list of its own saints, every church, parish diocese, ecclesiastical province, every religious institution and community in Poland has its particular heavenly patron. There are hundreds of saints, sometimes barely known to the rest of the world, but chosen for a particular reason. Sometimes a region is filled with shrines and statues of a particular saint because the saint had preached the gospel in the area, or had lived or died there. Perhaps miracles or visions of a particular saint had taken place there, or the virtues and attributes ascribed to the saint are cherished and particularly valued in that area. The choice of a specific saint depended on the saint's function as intercessor, benefactor, or protector. A saint might be the recognized intercessor with God for the alleviation of a particular need, the patron of something hoped for, or a protector against something fearful. Some saints are known as patrons of people suffering from a particular disease or problem, or become role models for certain occupations. The faithful turned to the saints to help them realize their hopes and protect them from what they feared.

St. Joseph

The oldest prayers in honor of St. Joseph in Poland come from the Wawel Benedictory in the 11th/12th century. They also appear in the 14th-century breviaries of the Kraków clergy, and in the 16th-century breviaries and offices especially of the Carmelite, Dominican, and Franciscan monasteries.

One of the oldest and main places of veneration of St. Joseph was the Carmelite Church in the city of Kalisz, consecrated in 1621, where St. Joseph was associated with an image of the Holy Family. According to tradition, a resident of the village of Szulec was healed due to the intervention of St. Joseph. In thanks, he made a votive offering of an image of the Holy Family and placed it in the church in Kalisz. It became known as St. Joseph of Kalisz (*Św. Józef Kaliski*). The painting was crowned with papal crowns on May 15, 1796. During the partitions of Poland when religious activities were curtailed, the cult of St. Joseph of Kalisz lessened, but was revived by the celebration of the 100th anniversary of the painting's coronation in 1896. The cult of St. Joseph of Kalisz grew again after World War II by pilgrimages of priests who had been prisoners in the Dachau concentration camp. While interned there, the priests, fearing the liquidation of the camp,

*St. Joseph of Kalisz. Photo courtesy of Narodowe Sankatarium
Św. Józefa w Kaliszu (National Sanctuary of St. Joseph in Kalisz)*

entrusted themselves to St. Joseph and vowed that if they survived, they would make pilgrimages to St. Joseph in Kalisz. The camp was liberated on April 29, 1945. Until the end of their lives, the clergy fulfilled their promise and made pilgrimages to Kalisz, thanking St. Joseph for being saved. The last of them, Fr. Leon Stępniak, died in 2013. In 2017, Pope Francis granted the Kalisz basilica the title of the National Shrine of St. Joseph.

Perhaps not as widely known as, for instance, the May devotions to the Blessed Virgin Mary, is that the whole month of March became dedicated to honoring St. Joseph. Initiated in Rome in 1810, this practice spread throughout the Catholic Church thanks to Pope Pius IX. In 1906, the printing house of Antoni Koziański from Kraków published a booklet titled "*Miesiąc marzec z przykładami poświęcony czci św. Józefa*" ("The month of March with examples devoted to the veneration of St. Joseph") which offered thirty days of reflection and examples of the glory and virtues of the saint. It is only one example of the numerous prayers, litanies, novenas as well as songs dedicated to his honor.

Shrine dedicated to St. Joseph, Tarnogód, Biłgoraj County.

Spirit of Place

St. Joseph is identified as the husband of the Blessed Virgin Mary, caretaker of the Christ Child, patron saint of carpenters, families, fathers, and those who work. He was considered to have special care of families and married couples. On his feast day of March 19th, widows and widowers of Poland often took their marriage vows. There was also a time in Poland when he was considered patron against temptations and was the saint to pray to for maintaining sobriety and restraint. He was also held to be the patron saint of a good death. The novena to St. Joseph is held to be an effective prayer in times of suffering, illness, anguish, crisis, or unemployment. He is turned to for enlightenment in difficult choices, healing, comfort and at the same time is a perfect mediator for expressing thanksgiving to God for favors received. He is also considered the caretaker of the Holy Church. Hundreds of churches in Poland bear his name and his image is seen frequently as an independent figure on posts and pillars along roadsides, but also in the interior of chapels in paintings or as a statue. St. Joseph is generally depicted holding the Infant Jesus on one arm and a white lily in the other.

St. John Nepomucen

St. John Nepomucen (*Św. Jan Nepomucen/Nepomuk*) is one of the most popular saints found on roadside shrines throughout all of Poland. Born in Nepomuc, Bohemia, near Prague, St. John used the name of his native town for his surname instead of his family name. He studied at the University of Prague, was ordained and became a canon. His rise in the church was meteoric. He was an ardent and zealous minister. He was appointed to the court of King Wenceslaus IV and unwillingly became a pawn in court politics and intrigues. It was his role as confessor to Queen Sophie, the king's beautiful young second wife, that became the cause of his death. The king tried to extort the confessions of his wife from St. John. When he refused to reveal what the queen had told him in confession, the king had him thrown in jail, racked, and burned with torches. After a second effort to extort the confessions of his wife from him, the king ordered that the martyr's hands and feet be bound and weighed down with rocks and that he be thrown from a bridge into the Moldau River in Prague in the middle of the night. It was said that the infamous deed was discovered when a heavenly light shone on the water where the body of St. John continued floating instead of sinking to the bottom. The year of his death was 1393. The cult of St. John Nepomucen began

Shrine to St. John Nepomucen, Chlewiska, Szydłowiec County.
Photo credit: Michał Zalewski

to spread in Prague soon after his tragic death. His burial place was considered a holy place, visited by the sick and the suffering. In succeeding years, numerous miracles were believed to have happened there and attempts to beatify him were successful.

Word about the martyr began to spread beyond Prague and Bohemia. He was canonized a saint in 1729 by Pope Benedict XIII and in central Europe his cult gained greater strength with the erection of statues and altars, the pressing of medals and the publishing of books and pamphlets about his life. The Jesuits promoted St. John Nepomucen throughout the known continents as the patron saint of a good confession.

In 1638, even before his beatification, a statue of St. John Nepomucen was erected on the Charles Bridge in Prague. Sculpted in wood by Jan Brokoff, a bronze copy of the original still adorns the Charles River. The figure depicts the saint standing in priest's clothes consist-

Spirit of Place

Statue of St. John Nepomucen, Rzeczyca Długa.

ing of a cassock, surplice, and stole, his head covered with a traditional priest's biretta and a nimbus of five stars surrounding the head. In one arm he cradles a crucifix and in the other holds a palm, the traditional symbol of martyrdom. It is this image that is the most widely reproduced of St. John Nepomucen throughout all of Poland, although one can occasionally encounter a more unusual form such as the saint kneeling or lying down in a death pose with closed eyes as if the artist was visualizing that night in 1393 when the saint was dying.

From Bohemia, the cult of St. John Nepomucen traveled quickly to neighboring Poland especially to the region of Dolny Śląsk (Lower Silesia), north of the border. This region hosts the richest and most interesting sculptures of St. John Nepomucen. One of the oldest dates back to 1704 and is located in Bystrzyca Kłodzka. At one time in the nearby village of Gorzanów, a few kilometers north of Bystrzyca Kłodzka, each year on the feast day of the saint on May 16, the community held a procession on water in his honor. The figure of St. John was placed on a barge, decorated with flowers, and allowed to float down the river that runs through the village. Behind the barge followed other boats filled with priests and local dignitaries. On the banks of the river the villagers lined up to throw fresh flowers at the barge as it passed by and sang religious songs. This tradition has now disappeared but the tributes to St. John Nepomucen in the form of wayside shrines and chapels continue throughout Poland to this day.

St. John Nepomucen is known as the patron saint of water, bridges, and farmers who have fields that they want to protect against floods. His statues are often found near wells and springs, watching that they not dry out. St. John Nepomucen also protected against water spirits that sat on the edges of ponds or rivers or under bridges in holes made by a flood. The water spirits were believed to lure careless passers-by into the water to drown them. If the nearby waters had a likeness of St. John, the demons lost their power and had to move someplace else. He is also considered the patron saint of drowning with his statue erected at sites of drowning. At the famous Wieliczka Salt Mine located outside of Kraków, there is a statue of St. John Nepomucen erected where there was a flood inside the mine and soldiers visiting the mine at the time lost their lives. He is patron saint of confessors and those who wish to control their tongue from excessive talking. For this reason, he is sometimes depicted with a finger against his lips in the traditional symbol of silence or sometimes holding a padlock. Sometimes he holds an open prayer book in both hands.

St. John's tomb is located in the cathedral in Prague, and he is the patron saint of the Czech Republic. Considering the number of shrines dedicated to this saint, however, it is clear he is also much loved and venerated in Poland. His feast day is celebrated on May 16. On this day, many communities gather at his shrine, bringing flowers and singing songs that memorialize the circumstances of St. John's death at the hands of Wenceslaus and recognizing him as a beloved guardian and patron.

St. Hedwig

St. Hedwig (*Św. Jadwiga Śląska*) was a woman who lived in the 13th century. Born in Bavaria, she was married to Henry I (*Henryk Brodaty*) of Silesia at a time when Poland consisted chiefly of separate kingdoms and there were constant feuds and wars. Despite Hedwig's wealthy state and marriage to a man who was king of Silesia, Kraków, and Great Poland, she lived a life of piety, poverty, and humility as mother to seven children and a caretaker of the poor. She always kept thirteen poor persons in her castle or with her as she traveled, feeding them and caring for their needs in honor of Christ and his apostles. Under the leadership of her husband, the region known as Śląsk (Silesia) prospered with the establishment of new towns with their own hospitals, churches, monasteries, and convents. Hedwig concerned herself greatly with alms houses and hospitals which she supported with her own money to provide food, clothing, and medicine. The legends say that even in winter, she would walk barefoot—her husband sent her a pair of shoes, insisting that she not be without them so she kept them under her arm. She established the convent at Trzebnica near Wrocław which, according to the wishes of the queen, was an educational institution to improve the condition of women. It began with a few women from a convent in Germany, who were then joined by Polish women. By the time of her death, there were over one hundred women at the convent. After the death of her husband, Hedwig completely renounced the world and entered the monastery of Trzebnica which she had founded. She died on October 15, 1243, and is venerated as a patroness of Poland. Her mortal remains were deposited at Trzebnica. She was canonized in 1266 by Clement IV, and her relics were enshrined the following year.

Late gothic bas-relief of St. Hedwig, Lower Silesia. Photo credit: Michał Zalewski

To recognize St. Hedwig in shrines throughout Poland, she is represented as either a woman dressed in the clothes of the Cistercian nuns, sometimes wearing a crown depicting her status, or barefoot with shoes in her hand; or she is shown as a noble lady holding a statue of the Virgin and Child, or holding a church (a symbol of a monastery); or holding a pair of shoes under arm. She is the patroness of Śląsk and so many wayside shrines in that region in particular are dedicated to her. She is also the patroness of Bavaria, brides, duchesses, marital problems, victims of jealousy, and widows. Her feast day is October 15.

Shrine dedicated to St. Kinga originally built in 1820, Nowy Korczyn, Busko County. Photo credit: Wikipedia

St. Kinga

Saint Kinga (1234-1292), also called Kunegunda or Cunegunda, belongs to the cadre of the most significant women of ancient Poland. Statues of her can be found throughout the Pieniny mountain region and especially around and in the cities of Nowy Sącz, Stary Sącz, and Kroscienko where she made her greatest contributions and impact.

The daughter of Hungarian king Beli IV and niece of St. Elizabeth of Hungary, Kinga was bethrothed to Bolesław Wstydliwy (the Shy) at the age of five, and as was the custom of the times, did not marry until later in her twelfth year. She was brought to Poland and lived under the tutelage of Salomea, later Blessed Salomea, who established in Poland the first religious order of Poor Clares under the rule of St. Francis of Assisi. The atmosphere in the court was a deeply religious one with Kinga attending Mass, praying several times a day in her chapel, and devoting a great deal of time caring for the poor. Living in this atmosphere of piety, Kinga resolved to offer her virgin state to God. In 1246, when she took her marriage vows, she persuaded her husband to live a life together in celibacy, to which he agreed, hence the name "the Shy" was given to Bolesław. In spite of the high status of being royalty, their beginning years were filled with difficulties. There were invasions by Mongol hordes who swept into the country murdering, pillaging, and leaving entire communities devastated. The couple had to flee Kraków, then the capital of Poland, and find refuge in other countries until they could safely return. Then there were disputes for the right to the throne and like a plague, additional attacks by the Mongols. One of their escapes from their attackers brought them to a smaller castle in Nowy Korczyn.

According to the local legend, a spring was said to have gushed forth at the bank of the Nida River in Nowy Korczyn, where the waters of that river ejected the body of the drowned Hungarian prince Andrzej, a refugee from his country who died at the hands of hired assassins in 1291. One day St. Kinga came to the source to wash her feet on the way to the church of St. Nicholas in Wiślica (currently non-existent). There she saw a child with an eye disease at the well. After wiping the child's eyes several times with water from the spring, the disease disappeared, an event that initiated the belief in the healing properties of the water. Pilgrims began gathering there, and the site was visited in particular by people with vision problems, in the hopes of being healed by the miraculous water. At the beginning of the 17th century, a chapel founded by nobleman Tomasz Borkowski was dedicated to Kinga and built in the form of an arch supported on four columns of limestone erected over the spring. After several decades it collapsed. Eventually, the spring was walled off and made into a well. In 1820 a new figure of St. Kinga was established there. She is considered patron saint of Nowy Korczyn and is honored every year there on her feast day of January 24 with a procession and prayers said at her feet.

When the Mongol hordes were finally beaten back, leaving entire communities empty and destroyed, Kinga apparently gave a substantial part of her jewels to her husband to rebuild the country. In return her husband deeded her land in the region of Stary Sącz.

It is this region which so honors her with numerous statues in roadside shrines. She directed the building of new churches and villages and became a mother to the people that inhabited them. She was mindful of a just and fair taxation, had a special place in her heart for orphans and widows, and gave particular attention to women who were pregnant and poor. She cared for the sick in their homes and in hospitals, often caring for their wounds herself. A queen of unusual virtue, goodness, and charity, she also actively participated in the attempts to canonize the bishop of Kraków, Stanislaus, who was martyred and who, indeed, was later named St. Stanislaus.

There are many legends surrounding Blessed Kinga and the discovery of salt mines in Poland. When Kinga was asked by her father what she would like as a wedding present, Kinga replied that she wanted something that could serve the people she was going to live with. She asked for salt. Determined to keep his promise, her father gave Kinga the Marmaros salt mine, the biggest and most prosperous salt deposits in Hungary. On her way to Poland, the princess visited the mine. She kneeled to pray next to the entrance and without warning suddenly threw her engagement ring inside. She gathered a group of the best Hungarian salt miners and told them to follow her to Poland. When the party arrived in Poland and was approaching Kraków, Kinga stopped and asked the miners to look for salt. They started digging and suddenly hit something very hard. It was a lump of salt. When they broke it open, hidden inside was Kinga's engagement ring. And that was how salt came to Poland. It is a much-loved legend in Poland. At the heart of the world renowned Wieliczka Salt Mine, named by UNESCO as a World Heritage Site, 101 meters deep, there is a magnificent chapel, the world's largest underground chapel, completely carved out of salt dedicated to her memory.

After the death of her husband in 1279 the widowed queen entered the Convent of the Nuns of the Order of Saint Clare, called the Poor Clares, in Stary Sącz which she herself had established and funded. There she embraced a daily life of work, fasting, and prayer. While in the convent she introduced the saying of prayers and singing songs in the Polish language and taught the other women to read and write. She took the veil in 1289, three years before her death, which was a difficult one, full of pain and suffering. Immediately after her death, people began to pray to her, and her grave became the sight of pilgrimages. In 1690 her beatification was announced by Pope Alexander III. In 1715 she was named a patron of Poland and Lithuania. In pictures she is depicted in the habit of the Poor Clares, holding a replica of the convent she established. She was canonized by Pope John Paul II in 1999. Her feast day is celebrated on the day of her death, July 24. She is the patron saint of salt miners and caretakers of the poor. She is also the patron of the diocese of Tarnów.

St. Barbara

St. Barbara was a young woman who was beheaded for refusing to deny her faith. The oldest evidence of the celebration of St. Barbara in Poland dates back to the 11th century. The Poor Clares of Kraków at the church of St. Andrew sung sequences (a hymn coming immediately before the Gospel in certain masses) in her honor. Prayers to St. Barbara from the 15th century ask for forgiveness of sins at the hour of death and acceptance of the Eucharist, protection against the devil, and to be ushered into heaven. She is considered the patron saint of a happy death.

Stone figure of St. Barbara erected at the turn of the 20th century, Wróblówce, Czarnej Dunajec region.
Photo credit: Panstwowe Museum Etnograficzne (National Ethnografic Museum in Warsaw)

The cult of St. Barbara became very strong in Poland during the 17th and 18th century when Poland was stricken with numerous epidemics and wars where sudden death was a continuous risk. There existed a Confraternity of St. Barbara in all of Poland during these centuries run by the Jesuits in Kraków. Among its members were kings, magnates, nobles, burghers, and regular townspeople. Also among its members was St. Stanislaus Kostka. It is said that when on his deathbed, the landlord refused to allow a chaplain with the Holy Eucharist to enter, but instead St. Stanislaus had a vision where St. Barbara appeared to him with Holy Communion.

St. Barbara is also patron saint to fishermen and anyone who works on rivers or plies the sea. In olden times in Mazowsze, her image could be found on the masthead of boats and barges and no sailor or deckhand would leave land without her image on their person. During the reign of August II (called Mocny, or Strong) in the 17th century, in the church of the Blessed Virgin Mary in Warsaw, fishermen and their entire families attended masses in the morning and evening of her feast day and distributed fish to the poor. Because of her close association with water, her image appears in numerous churches and wayside chapels and shrines in the Pomorze (Pomerania) district along the Baltic Sea coast.

St. Barbara is also considered the patron saint of stone, coal, metal, and salt miners. Prayers to her begin with "St. Barbara, patroness of the brotherhood of miners, protect us on the ground and under the ground ..." Her image can frequently be found near mines along the Carpathians where the extraction of metals and ore has been a tradition since the 15th century. Many wayside shrines in the heavy coal and ore mining industries in Śląsk (Silesia) are also devoted to her. During World War II, St. Barbara became the patron saint of many units of the Polish underground army who fought against the Nazis. Her feast day, December 4, is celebrated by miners throughout all of Poland. In the Wieliczka Salt Mine, listed by UNESCO (United Nations Educational, Scientific and Cultural Organization) as one of the most remarkable sites in the world, her feast day is celebrated by miners with a mass in the chapel of St. Kinga. Her image on many banners during processions depicts St. Barbara wearing a wide cloak covering miners, or St. Barbara with a hammer and pick axe. In statues and paintings, St. Barbara may be depicted in a variety of ways: carrying the sacramental cup and wafer; with a tower, in which she was confined before her beheading; with a sword, the instrument of her death, and holding a green palm.

St. Florian

Relics of St. Florian have belonged to the city of Kraków since the 11th century when a church was raised in his name in the Kleparz district of the city. Legend has it that when a major fire began to destroy most of Kraków, the church was untouched. His cult spread throughout the country and he became the patron of those in danger from fire. Fires were frequent in the countryside of old Poland. Wooden houses with thatched roofs and stables full of hay, as well as cooking over open fires both indoors and out, contributed to frequent fires. The statue of St.

Statue of St. Florian in Krzyżanowice, Radom County.

St. Florian at Florian Gate entrance to Old Town in Kraków.
Photo credit: Wikipedia

Florian was generally erected in the middle of a village or town square with the church steeple or tower of the town hall serving as the lookout from which firemen watched for fires. He is usually depicted dressed in a soldier's uniform (Roman) carrying a bucket to douse the fire. Sometimes there is a burning house at his feet. St. Florian is also the patron saint of many cities and towns where his image is found on the coat-of-arms. His feast day is celebrated on May 4th.

Statue of St. Nicholas,
Słupanowo, Szamotuły County.
Photo credit: Michał Zalewski

St. Nicholas

Nikolaos of Myra (*Św. Mikolaj*)
was a historic 4th-century saint
and bishop of Myra in what is
modern-day Turkey. The his-
torical Saint Nicholas is remembered and revered among Catholic
and Orthodox Christians in many countries throughout Eastern Europe and Greece. When Vladimir the Great brought Christianity to
Russia in 988 AD, he also brought stories of Saint Nicholas, who became Russia's most beloved saint. The cult of St. Nicholas traveled to
Poland through the trade routes from the Baltic Sea and through the
Pomorze region of Poland, and via land routes from the east to all the
major cities of Poland. The first churches carrying his name arose in
the 12th century in Poznań and by the 13th and 14th centuries every

seventh church in the Poznań diocese was named after St. Nicholas. By 1880, there were over thirty churches as well as innumerable chapels and wayside shrines dedicated to this saint in the Pomorze region.

Because he was known to have calmed the sea during a violent storm, he is considered the patron saint of those who work on barges, ferry boat operators, sailors, and fisherman, and his image sometimes has a background containing ships. As the patron saint of children, he may be depicted with three figures climbing out of a wooden barrel in reference to the three slaughtered children he resurrected. In Poland St. Nicholas is more revered as the patron saint of shepherds, cattle, horses, and sheep. His feast day, December 6, falls during a time when wolves who roamed the countryside did great damage to both humans and livestock.

In Roman Catholic iconography Saint Nicholas is portrayed as a bishop, wearing a red bishop's cloak, red miter, and crozier. He is often depicted as a bishop with wolves at his feet. Because of his reputation for helping impoverished girls find dowries so they could marry, the image may show him holding in his hand three purses, three coins, or three balls of gold. In parts of Poland where the Russian orthodox faith gained a foothold, he is depicted as an Orthodox bishop, wearing the omorphion and holding a gospel book.

St. Roch

St. Roch is the patron saint against pestilence and epidemics for humans and farm animals. In the Kurpie region of Poland on the Feast of St. Roch (August 16th), protector of cattle and friend of dogs, the parishioners brought gifts from nature to the altar in the form of bundles of wheat and flax and flowers. In bygone days, people brought candles of their own making to which were attached small figures of home animals also made from wax as votive offerings. After the mass, the parishioners processed out to a pasture beyond the village where sheep, cattle, and horses had been gathered. A bonfire was lit burning the green branches of the juniper bush with the addition of herbs blessed on Corpus Christi, and the animals were driven through the gusts of smoke—first the sheep, then the cattle, then the horses—as a way of protecting them. During the entire proceeding, a drum kept up a steady beat. At the conclusion, the priest blessed the animals with holy water, concluding the event.

Legend has it that on getting sick himself, St. Roch did not receive

the same kind of mercy that he was known for showing to others from the townspeople among whom he found himself. They kicked him out of town. St. Roch built himself a hut in the forest, next to which sprouted a small spring from which he drew water. He only lacked food. A dog befriended him and would come running to him every day. Not only did the dog bring him a loaf of bread, but he also licked his wounds. In the iconography of St. Roch, he is depicted as a young pilgrim with a walking staff or as a beggar in rags; or with a dog holding a loaf of bread in its mouth or licking his wounds or running next to him.

St. Rosalia

St. Rosalia (*Św. Rozalia*) is also invoked in times of plagues and pestilence. Born in the 12th century to a wealthy family in Sicily, Rosalia was devoutly religious and, against her father's wishes, vowed not to marry. On the eve of her engagement at age fourteen, Rosalia secretly left everything and took refuge in a mountain cave and lived as a hermit. She fed on forest undergrowth, cactus fruit, chestnuts, roots, and spring water. She led a life of penance and austerities. On the walls of the cave, she carved the inscription: "I, Rosalia, the daughter of God, decided to live here for the love of Christ."

Shrine to St. Rosalia built in 1536, Sławków near Katowice and close-up of nearby granite stone giving the history of the shrine (see translation next page). Photo credit: Wikipedia

In 1624, a plague beset Palermo. During this hardship St. Rosalia reportedly appeared to a hunter, to whom she indicated where her remains were to be found. She ordered him to bring her bones to Palermo and have them carried in procession through the city. The hunter did what she had asked. After her remains were carried around the city three times, the plague ceased. The grateful inhabitants of Palermo chose Rosalia as the patron saint of the city and since then she has been called upon as the patron saint who protects against plague and contagious diseases. Depictions of St. Rosalia often include a skull, a symbol of her lost remains. In one of her hands, she may be portrayed as holding a crucifix, or sometimes lilies as a symbol of her chastity.

A shrine in the form of a pillar, built in 1536, is the oldest of many wayside shrines in Sławków. Located there at one time was a cross, a symbol of the suffering of Christ, which was replaced with a pillar dedicated to St. Rosalia. The stone cross at its peak with the date 1630 carved across its horizontal beam marks the occasion of its renovation. A plaque, also from that same date, situated in the upper half of the pillar commemorates the epidemic that hit the city at the same time. The shrine underwent another a renovation in 1896. On August 24, 2006, it was entered in the register of monuments. After re-restoration, it was consecrated on September 6, 2009. A nearby granite stone helps passers-by understand its significant history:

Shrine dedicated to St. Rosalia
Ancient pillar of the Suffering Christ
from 1536
Renovated in 1630
—The inscription from the 17th century

Inspired by the heavens, night time prayers,
Christians renewed this pillar of the Lord's Passion
this year, hunger and plague lasted throughout the year
many people complained dying of hunger,
eating various grasses and vile things.
This year, a basket of rye cost eight złotys.
1630

Statue of St. Anthony of Padua, Zwiartów, Tomaszów Lubelski County.
Photo credit: Michał Zalewski

St. Anthony of Padua

St. Anthony of Padua (*Św. Antoni Padewski*) is the patron saint of innumerable churches, parishes, and sanctuaries all over Poland, and it is estimated that over 198 towns derive their name from the name of St. Anthony. There is hardly a church in Poland without an altar or a statue of this saint, not to mention all the roadside figures and chapels that are dedicated to him. The chapel of St. Anthony, carved in salt in Wieliczka, is one of the oldest chapels in the mine dating to the 17th century. The first mass was said in the chapel in 1698 for the miners, who also took him on as a patron because they searched for "white gold," i.e., salt.

St. Anthony proved to be an excellent preacher and a person with deep theological knowledge. He began to preach the word of God earnestly as an itinerant preacher. He is usually invoked in finding lost or stolen things. "*Św. Antoni, dopomóż odszukać koni!*" ("St. Anthony help us find our horse!") is an old proverb/prayer that was invoked with lost (or sometimes stolen) horses.

The history of praying to St. Anthony for lost items can be traced back to an incident in Anthony's own life when he had lost a book of psalms that was very important to him for teaching students in his Franciscan order. A novice who had grown tired of living the religious life decided to depart the community and also took Anthony's psalter with him. Upon realizing his psalter was missing, Anthony prayed it would be found or returned to him. The novice was contrite and was moved to return the psalter to Anthony and returned to the Order as well. Shortly after his death, people began praying through Anthony to find or recover lost and stolen articles.

St. Anthony of Padua is generally depicted in a brown Franciscan habit, having taken vows with the Franciscan order who spread his popularity throughout Poland. He is typically portrayed holding the child Jesus (who was to have appeared to him) in his arms, or a lily (symbol of a pure life devoted to God), or a book (he was canonized as a Doctor of the Church), or all three. His feast day is celebrated on June 13.

St. Stanislaus Szepanowski

St. Stanislaus Szepanowski (*Św. Stanisław ze Szepanowa*), bishop of Kraków and martyr, fell into conflict with King Bolesław II, known as the Bold (reigned 1076-1079) who ordered his death. Stanislaus was slain while saying mass in the Kraków church in 1079, now known as Basilica of St. Michael the Archangel and St. Stanislaus. His martyrdom resulted in canonization in 1253 and his cult began to spread to all parts of Poland but especially in Małopolska (Little Poland) where tradition says he was born in 1030. He is the patron of the archdioceses of Warsaw, Kieliec, Płock, Sandomierz, and Tarnów and is depicted wearing pontifical robes and a crowned eagle. During the times of the partitions, St. Stanislaus became the symbol of a united and independent Poland. He, along with St. Adalbert (Św. Wojciech), patron saint of Gniezno with numerous chapels and shrines erected along the route where he stopped to preach, and St. Florian, were named the patron saints of Poland.

* * *

The list of different saints is endless but each is venerated as a reminder of someone who had received God's grace. Each region, each town, each individual heart is unique as to whom it wishes to honor. A few other figures who are often seen in roadside shrines include:

St. Therese de Lisieux, a Carmelite nun portrayed with roses entwining a crucifix.

St. Francis of Assisi in monk's robes with animals and birds.

St. Francis Xavier usually wears a black cassock with a white surplice and stole. The cross was one of the most important symbols of Xavier's missionary activity. He is often depicted preaching or baptizing while holding a cross.

Statue of St. Francis Xavier, Opatowiec in Świętokrzyskie region.

Interior of chapel dedicated to St. Maximilian Kolbe, the Franciscan priest murdered in Auschwitz, Niemil, Tomaszów Lubelski region.

St. Isidore, patron saint of farmers.

St. Onufry, patron saint of pilgrims and travelers, is venerated as Saint Onuphrius in both the Roman Catholic and Eastern Catholic churches.

St. Giles (Idzi) is the patron saint to pray to in the event of infertility as well as patron saint of the sick experiencing mental diseases, epilepsy, leprosy, and disabilities.

St. Bartholomew, patron saint of beekeepers, was especially popular in the Kurpie region and on his feast day of August 24 honey was collected from the hives.

And in recent years more contemporary saints have begun to appear:

St. Maximilian Marie Kolbe, Franciscan monk murdered by the Nazis in Auschwitz in 1941.

Interior of chapel dedicated to St. Pope John Paul II, Kałuszynie.
Photo credit: Krystyna Bartosik

St. Pope John Paul II, the Catholic world's first Polish pope and builder of bridges with other faiths. Hundreds of churches and roadside shrines have been raised in St. Pope John Paul II's honor throughout Poland.

CHAPTER 4
Art & Artists

When we look at the vast array of the tens of thousands of different roadside chapels, figures, and crosses, the paintings that decorate them, the larger and small wooden figures, the stone statuary as well as metal crosses, we know that behind the sentiment of an individual who wished to erect a chapel or a cross, there had to be someone who could help execute the vision. Who was the stonemason who carved the stone cross or built the foundation for the shrine? Who were the artists who carved the wooden image of the Sorrowing Christ or stone statue of St. Florian? Who painted the Madonna so beautifully? Who were the carpenters and joiners, sculptors, painters, woodcarvers, blacksmiths, and foundry workers who took the vision and made it a reality?

What can sometimes be found on roadside shrines is the name of the individual or group who commissioned the work as well as the date and the intent or reason it was erected. What is rare to find are the names of the artists. Some of the works of professionals were signed. Of those created by folk artists, not so much. Unless the names of the individuals responsible for hammering out a cross or carving a figure was entered into parish records, the creators are generally unknown.

For a long time in Poland there existed two very separate and distinct socioeconomic classes of people: the very rich and the very poor. The rich, chiefly nobles and church officials, were able to commission established artisans and master craftsmen to fulfill their vision for a chapel or shrine. Based on the times and styles that were prevalent, they chose elaborate and decorative figures for their chapels and shrines and were able to hire professional woodcarvers, masons, blacksmiths, and painters. These professionals trained for years at a studio or workshop, received their master status and could call themselves master craftsman. Very often the professional craftsman lived in the house of the noble who commissioned a particular work until his work was completed. Proud of his endeavors on behalf of the rich and famous, the craftsman may have signed his name to the completed work.

It wasn't until the emancipation of the serfs in the 19th century and the development of a prospering peasantry that a peasant could afford to hire a qualified stone carver to carve figures into the base or sides of a pillar, a blacksmith to hammer out a metal cross, or a woodcarver to carve a small statue for the front of their home. The development of a middle class increased trade, communication, travel, and the establishment of churches and more roadside shrines. Where previously five or six villages were forced to travel miles to the nearest church, smaller towns now began to build their own churches. As a result, master craftsmen came to the more rural areas as they were needed to build huge edifices such as a church and then complete its interior with altars, pulpits, and statuary. This brought in carpenters, joiners, masons, experts in stained glass, and other artisans. The master craftsman would take up residence in a village and either bring apprentices with him or took on local apprentices. When their work was done, the entire studio of artists and craftsmen changed their location in search of new work or followed a commission to build a new altar or carve figures in another town or region. The apprentices moved along with their masters to the next commission or stayed on in their own villages and became the next generation of craftsmen available to local individuals.

There were also a number of artisans who were self-taught, who may have keenly observed the work of an expert and were good with their hands. They worked alone with simple tools they had made themselves or that were made by a blacksmith. They had their own ideas and techniques. Each contact with the outside world, each creative attempt provided the opportunity to discover new motifs and patterns and subsequently enrich the landscape of Poland with a wide array of different styles and techniques of roadside shrines. This was true for woodcarvers, stonemasons, and for those who molded in clay and for those whose medium was paint.

WOODCARVERS

Adam Chętnik, the recognized ethnographer of the Kurpie region of Poland wrote: "Long ago in the Kurpie region there were many home-grown woodworkers — those who whittled crosses, religious figures, and entire altars — carving and whittling from their own drawings and imagination." In the Kurpie region, these homespun artists were called *bogorobów*. In other regions of Poland they were called *świątkarze*, both words referring to holy image makers.

Some of these carvers and sculptors were initially carpenters, joiners, or wheelwrights who had a working knowledge of the properties of wood and turned their hand to carving religious objects. Some

began as little boys, tending cows or sheep in the meadow, passing the time carving small animals and then graduating up to small figures for the Christmas crèche and then larger figures suitable for shrines. These folk artists lived in the village but during free time took a knife to wood and whittled a small cross or figure of some saint seen previously in church or on a holy card. Many had working farms, which required a great deal of labor from sun up to sun down, and carved only in the winter when they had free time. For others, where the land was poor and individuals could barely eke out an existence, or poor health prevented them from earning income through farming, carving religious figures and crosses became the major source of livelihood. Many were deeply devout individuals who perceived their work as a tribute and glory to God and as a way of thanking Him for his care.

Each folk artist had his own particular style rarely using more than a small sharp knife and small block of linden wood, which lent itself to carving. Some of the artists used special carving chisels made by the local blacksmith. Other tools included planes and hand-powered drills, while larger images required a hatchet or saw. Besides linden wood, aspen, alder and even resinous pine were used to carve the figures.

The inspiration for many religious figures were to be found in their local church, prayer books, or a holy picture brought back from pilgrimage by someone in the village or even from existing roadside shrines. Some preferred a particular motif that was close to their hearts such as the Sorrowing Christ or the Pieta. Whatever the source of their inspiration, they took it and transformed it through their own particular artistry. Sometimes artists took their work to the local church fair or festival where the faithful bought their statues and holy pictures. Sometimes their work was entrusted to peddlers. Some refused to take money for their work, citing that "only Judas sold Jesus for silver." Instead, they took something in barter. The work of these folk artists often found their way to the home altars or small shrines attached to a house or a tree. Sometimes a craftsman's ability and artistry was noted by the parish priest, who would order a Madonna or crucifix for inside the church.

A few of the better-known wood sculptors in Poland were:

Andrzej Wawro (also known as Jędrzej Wowro) was born in 1864 in the village of Gorzeń Dolny near Wadowice. Andrzej was not given school education and remained illiterate his whole life, obtaining his education from everyday life, church sermons, and then, thanks to his first wife, from stories about saints. He worked in a mine, a paper mill, helped on other farms, and was even a gravedigger. When time and circumstances allowed, he would take out his penknife and carve. Andrzej Wawro was primarily a sculptor. He created figures of Christ, Mary, and the saints. He often decorated his works with floral motifs, birds and angels. He also had a short episode with graphics and made wood blocks, also with a religious theme.

Folk sculptor Andrzej Wawro, with carvings of Sorrowing Christ at bottom of photo, 1939.

Photo credit: Narodowe Archiwum Cyfrowe

Paweł Bryliński was born in 1814 in Wieruszów, on the border of Małopolska and Wielkopolska, into a family of craftsmen. As a sculptor, he was probably self-taught, although it is believed that he developed his talent under the guidance of his uncle, a woodcarver from Wieruszów. He lived the life of a wandering sculptor. With the arrival of spring, he left home with a cart full of tools. During his work, he usually lived with whoever commissioned him to establish a cross. For material, he used mainly thick oak beams, less often pine, decorating the vertical beam with astoundingly beautiful carved figures. His most common iconographic theme was Holy Week with sculptures of Saint Mary Magdalene, the mother of God, and Saint John the Evangelist and he embellished his works with polychrome, using vivid colors. He painted not only the

Images of St. Anthony and St. Lawrence on the vertical beam of a cross carved by Paweł Bryliński in Nabyszyce.
Photo credit: Wikipedia

characters' clothes, but also emphasized the features of the face with color. In the course of several decades of activity, Bryliński developed his own style, allowing for easy distinction of the works that came from his hand. They are characterized by great realism of the presented figures, abundant decoration, and careful detailing.

Wojciech Kułach "Wawrzyńcok" (1812-1897) is the most famous folk sculptor of the 19th century in Podhale. He was born on March 24, 1812, in Gliczarów, and died in 1897. During his lifetime

Carving of St. Florian by artist Wojciech Kulach in second half of 19th century, Muzeum Etnograficzne im, Seweryna Udzieli w Krakowie.

Photo credit: Marcin Wąsik

he apparently made a walking pilgrimage to Rome, the result of which was a collection of drawings, sketches, and studies on sculpture. He carved in wood and stone, as well as in metal. The culmination of his work are three altars in an old church in Zakopane at Kościeliska Street.

Boxed shrine of Christ in the Garden by Michał Gier, c. 1920.

Photo credit: Marcin Wąsik

Michał Gier lived in the years 1853-1929 and came from the town of Rybna (Kraków region), and he was one of the most original self-taught sculptors. For many years, he made numerous sculptures for rural folk who wanted to establish a shrine. He often did not take any money for his work, and was rewarded with food and shelter. His work evolved to a high level of distinctive expression.

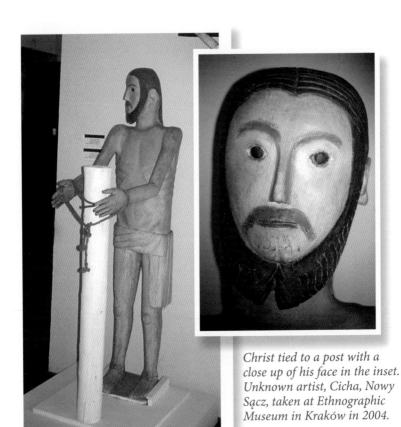

Christ tied to a post with a close up of his face in the inset. Unknown artist, Cicha, Nowy Sącz, taken at Ethnographic Museum in Kraków in 2004.

* * *

Small town or rural village woodcarvers often worked alone without seeing someone else's rendering of the same image, but there were situations where family members took up carving as well. While a brother-in-law or nephew would have their own particular skills, the close connection had an influence on their work and certain "schools" developed. One such "school" existed in the Rzeszów district called Sanok. In the Sanok school, the Sorrowing Christ is presented with a cloak over his shoulders which is pinned at the neck with a clasp or buckle. The front of the figure is entirely exposed. A large head with a crown of thorns is supported by both palms resting on the knees. The use of both arms to support the head is very unusual in the Sorrowing Christ and tends to be identified as being carved or influenced by the Sanok school. In addition, the legs are thin with large feet in these renditions.

In the Krosno region, while there were wide variations, the Sorrowing Christ is depicted without a cloak and covered only by a loin cloth. The manner of sculpting the hair, the slender torso that gradually increases to wide hips and the clearly delineated knots at the back to indicate a spinal column, identifies it as originating from this area. In the Lublin region, the torso is more muscular, the legs wide apart. The most prominent feature is the face, and the head is crowned with thorns. Moving north towards Mazowsze, the Sorrowing Christ is without a cloak, only a loin cloth and crown of thorns, the body slender and elongated. In the Kurpie region, the entire figure of the Sorrowing Christ is clothed in a habit, as if a monk, with the entire torso covered and tied at the waist with a rope and only the bare feet visible. This type of rendering of the Sorrowing Christ traveled from Kurpie to neighboring Podlesie. In the Kashubian region, the Christ figures are similar to Silesia but without a cape and a skull beneath his feet and holding a reed-scepter.

With the passage of centuries, many of the early shrines and carved wooden figures have been lost forever. Weather-worn from their forest or roadside niches, many have crumbled. Some have been lost to theft. To protect them from both fates, many of the oldest sacred images carved in wood have been removed from the roadside for preservation in national and regional museums.

STONE CUTTERS/CARVERS

There were numerous stone-cutting/carving centers throughout Poland including the regions of Kraków, Tarnów, and Kielce where limestone was abundant. Jozefów in the Zamość region was another stone-cutting/carving center, as was Bruśno in the Lubaczów district. There were entire regions where extracting and cutting stone was the major industry, and the craft of stone carving was passed down through the generations. Many stonemasons began as woodcarvers who were able to cross over to stone as their medium. Stone cutting and carving were essential to the process of building roads and the exterior as well as the interior of churches, especially the intricately carved portals, numerous altars, and baptismal and holy water fonts. Master craftsmen also carved large mausoleums, sarcophagi, and intricate figures as grave markers for those that could afford such work. These larger edifices, interior structures, and figures were documented in parish records or the artist sometimes carved his name and date into the work.

Polish ethnographers recognize the most abundant region for stone carvings and folk art made of stone was southern and southeastern Poland along the Carpathian range where sandstone was abundant. The villages in the region of Jasło and Gorlice produced many folk stone carvers. One of the richest centers of stone carving identified by Polish ethnographers in this region is the town of Bartne in the Gorlice district in southeastern Poland.

At one time this region was inhabited by an ethnic group of individuals known as Lemki. The Lemki were an early nomadic tribe who traveled along the Carpathians from Stary Sącz all the way to the Bieszczady Mountains looking for grazing ground for their sheep in the uninhabited or thinly populated valleys. They

Shrine carved from stone, Mników, 1925, Muzeum Etnograficzne im, Seweryna Udzieli w Krakowie.
Photo credit: Leopold Węgrzynowicz

were a mixed group of eastern Slavs and Vlachs (Romanians) who later mixed with Poles as the region became more populated. The Lemki became very proficient stone cutters, mining their stone from the mountain of Magurycz Wielki.

First and foremost, the stone cutters produced utilitarian objects critical to the livelihood of the town or village: items such as millstones for grinding grain and whetstones for sharpening axes and knives, as well as basic gravestones and markers for the cemetery. The abundant soft and fine-grained sandstone in the region was also used to make roadside crosses and wayside shrines with figures. Roughly cut to the approximate size of the sculpture, the stone was transported on sledges or horse carts to the stone-cutter's yard. The stone carvers worked in open air using points, hammers, and various chisels forged by the local blacksmith. They carved the base of the pillars for roadside shrines in bas-relief, the smaller statues, and/or carved the major stone figure on top of the pedestal or pillar. Sometimes entire

Spirit of Place

Shrine carved from stone with inset showing close-up of Pieta bas-relief sculpted from stone in one of the niches, Piorunka, Nowy Sącz region, c.1918-1934. Photo credit: Narodowe Archiwum Cyfrowe

small wayside chapels were hewed from local sandstone. These were fairly primitive square blocks of stone with a small niche for a picture or figure. There were even those where the entire body of the chapel, complete with roof, cupola, and cross, were hewn from a single piece of stone. Transport of the chapel to the designated site was completed under tremendous difficulty with the help of numerous pairs of oxen. Smaller items such as crucifixes for insertion into a niche in a roadside shrine or for home altars were also produced. The range of trade in their products extended to Lwów, Zamość, and Kolbuszowa but the traditional place of sale was the church fair in Jarosław.

Shrine made from a solid block of sandstone, Wierochomla, Piwniczna-Zdrój region, c. 1918-1934. Photo credit: Narodowe Archiwum Cyfrowe (National Digital Archives)

World events, especially the destruction of Poland during WWII, caused many of the stone-carving centers to close. Many of the stone masons were killed. Many who had farmed as well as carved in their spare time moved to the west of Poland to begin there over again and others went to the mines in Silesia. The production of stone crosses and figures dwindled. The availability of new products such as plaster of paris also changed the face of many wayside shrines and chapels.

POTTERS

Archeological digs in Poland reveal that by the 7th century AD, the craft of pottery began making headway in such places as Poznań, Gniezno, and Kalisz. During these early times, pots and vessels were being made from slabs of flattened clay. At the turn of the 19th into the 20th century, potters' workshops operated in more than nine hundred localities throughout Poland. In greater Poland, the center of pottery making was in Poznań and its surrounding areas. There were also potters in the Pultusk, Biłgoraj, Nowy Sącz, and Lublin regions. Potters from major towns as well as village potters chiefly made functional, indispensable items for the home. Housewives needed pitchers to serve buttermilk. They needed jugs and jars for preserving meats, fruits, and vegetables through the long winter, and flowerpots for their geraniums kept on the windowsill. Some potters made specialty items such as clay pipes for the men who enjoyed their tobacco, and children's toys like clay whistles and birds that were sold at church fairs. Others made the small holy water containers hung by the entrance door to the home.

Eventually clay pottery for cooking began to be replaced by factory-made cast-iron pots. Enamelware also became popular. These items lasted longer and tended not to break or crack as readily as something ceramic. In the 1930s the pottery industry in Poland seriously began to decline and rather than making functional items for the home, many potters turned to making specialty items such as ceramic tiles, flower vases, and decorative pitchers. Some potters focused primarily on making small figures. Iłża in the Kielce district became famous for its artists who constructed award-winning ceramic figurines as did Medyna Głogowska in the Rzeszów district. The figures made out

Clay figure of Sorrowing Christ, artist unknown, 2009. Private possession.

of clay were of three types: animals (for children to play with such as sheep, birds, and chickens that were often made into whistles); scenes from the life of a village (woman carrying a butter churn, woman with a basket); and holy images (such as a crucifix, various saints, Christ on the Cross). Unlike vases and pots where a mound of clay was thrown and formed on a potter's wheel, most figures were built slowly by hand, molding the head, torso, feet and arms, garments, and any other props necessary for identifying the image. Simple tools were used to cut the clay and to make details such as eyes and hair. The most widely used decorative element in figurines was to obtain contrast by using various clays which gave off different colors after firing or through the use of glazes. Copper sulfate gave a green color, ferrous oxide produced a yellow cast, and manganese dioxide resulted in a brown color.

Besides an individual figure or likeness of a saint or the Blessed Mother, potters made small chapels of the shadow box kind. Flat slabs of clay were used to build a base or platform, side walls, and a roof. Inside would be a scene from the life of Christ such as Christ in the Tomb, the Pieta, the Sorrowing Christ, or one of the saints. The firing of such a hand-built sculpture created one single piece of work that encompassed the figure or figures and the structure to display it. These items were made for the local villagers but were also meant to be small souvenirs for town buyers on market day, or to be sold at the innumerable church fairs that took place throughout all of Poland or at pilgrimage sites where everyone wanted a reminder of their journey. These were items that could be placed on the table that served as the home altar or in the niche on the outer wall of a home.

Of the nine hundred potters' workshops that existed at the end of the 19th century, fewer than three hundred fifty were operating in 1950. By 1970 there were fewer than two hundred. For instance, in Pultusk in 1914, there were approximately twenty potters' workshops. By the end of World War II, there were barely four. Today many of the figures found in roadside shrines are cast from gypsum.

PAINTERS AND ILLUSTRATORS

In response to Martin Luther's criticism of the corruption within the Roman Catholic Church with its sale of indulgences, pilgrimages, and excessive veneration of saints, the Catholic Church launched its own aggressive response, especially when it came to the veneration of saints. In 1621, the Kraków synod of bishops decreed that copies of miraculous images, in particular Our Lady of Częstochowa, should only be painted on the site of the original, to "its image and likeness." It also recommended that other paintings representing the Lord and the saints should also be worshipped, and in particular, care should be taken that they adorn roadside shrines and crosses. This synodal decree of setting images on roadside shrines was faithfully carried out and led to the mass production of religious paintings which were then bought by the faithful. Going on a pilgrimage to a holy site and having paintings representing Christ, the Virgin Mary, and the saints was public evidence of one's piety and faith.

The city of Częstochowa played a large role in the production and distribution of religious paintings. The Pauline Fathers, keepers of the miraculous original painting of Our Lady of Częstochowa at the monastery of Jasna Góra, had their own painting center for painting the image of Our Lady. The monastery provided patterns for paint-

The most widely depicted and universally recognized image of Our Lady Of Częstochowa, also known as the Black Madonna.
Photo credit: Wikipedia

ing and kept strict control over the quality and prices. Painters made many large paintings commissioned by the wealthy for church interiors and also painted the interior walls of the smaller wayside chapels. Many of the miniature chapels were outfitted with frescoes, paintings, and numerous figures and crucifixes on the altars. The Jasna Góra monastery hired enough painters, workers, and laborers associated with production to keep the masses of pilgrims who came to the shrine well supplied with images to take home for their home altars or for placement in the shrines. The painters' guilds kept strict control, forbidding sales by any renegade painters and required stamping of paintings as being guild made.

Pilgrims were able to purchase copies of the Black Madonna at whatever price they could afford at the merchant stalls lining the slope of Jasna Góra. Other holy pictures available were the Sacred Heart, the Blessed Mother, and the Last Supper. Equally popular were paintings of the flight of the holy family into Egypt or depictions of the various saints. Merchants from Częstochowa also wandered all over Greater Poland selling goods at church fairs and local markets.

The painting center in Częstochowa did not remain exclusive for long. The painting arts especially grew and developed in other pilgrimage centers, with religious-themed paintings produced on board and canvas. Bolima near Łowicz and Skulsk near Kalisz became well known for their religious oil paintings. The mountain region of Podhale produced richly-colored paintings on glass of the crucifixion, the Holy Family, and the saints for household and wayside shrines. The control measures set up by the painters' guilds, could not stop the rise of smaller workshops with lesser skills from setting up stalls leading to pilgrimage centers and selling their work cheaply. Nor could they stop the emergence of primitive or folk painters who spent the entire winters painting and then took to the road in the summer to sell their work themselves. Eventually workshops engaged in mass production of religious artifacts that were sold by itinerant salesmen called *obraznicy* who, as their name implies (from *obraz* – picture), specialized in selling religious paintings and pictures and could be seen traveling throughout old Poland with their wares. Able to reach even the remotest villages their products were bought up locally for home altars and wayside shrines.

Black and white woodcut image of Sorrowing Christ, Jędrzej Wawro, c. 1925-1933. Photo credit: *Muzeum Etnograficzne im. Seweryna Udzieli w Krakowie*

Cardboard began to appear in the second half of the 19th century. In later years less expensive forms of holy pictures in the form of black and white woodcuts were produced by the Jesuit printing houses. These black and white paper holy pictures were cheaper than those painted on glass, wood, or canvas, and subsequently enjoyed greater popularity. Many country roadside shrines were more simple affairs requiring only a flat image or picture of Christ,

Wooden cross with figure of Christ painted on sheet metal, Nowica, Wrocław region. Photo credit: Michał Zalewski

Our Lady of Częstochowa, or a saint. This could be a woodcut or a lithograph. These lent themselves especially to the small, private little box shrines attached to a house wall or a tree in front of the farm or meadow.

Another form of painting was that of painting on sheet metal. The development of non-ferrous metallurgy after the mid-19th century in Poland led to the production of durable sheets of sheet metal. Crosses cut out of sheet metal with a painted figure of the crucified Christ appeared on the roads at the turn of the 18th and 19th centuries. They were generally small figures of Christ crucified on metal crosses placed on brick plinths. As production increased and prices for the metal dropped, much larger images began to be cut and attached to existing wooden crosses. This style of crosses can be seen in regions of Wrocław and Lower Silesia and rarely in other parts of Poland.

BLACKSMITHS AND
DECORATIVE IRONWORK

The earliest crosses and shrines were made of wood from the numerous forests that filled the landscape of Poland, but eventually they decayed or were lost due to weather. In 1900, ethnographer Zygmunt Gloger wrote: "During the winter of 1880, huge winds of hurricane proportions passed over parts of Poland knocking down the old wooden crosses. Edicts by the government at that time forbade fixing them so any new ones that were erected were made of metal and set in stone."

Iron had always been a very expensive commodity in old Poland. Entire homes were built complete with furnishings without the use of a single nail. The expense of iron was limited to latches for doors and metal parts and fittings used in plows, sleighs, buggies, and wagons that were so essential to a working farm. Iron on chapels and shrines made by a village blacksmith did not come into wide use in Poland until the second half of the 19th century with the emancipation of the peasants and improvement in their economic situation.

The most visible artistry of the blacksmith in Poland is seen chiefly in shrines and chapels in the form of metal crosses. There were two types of crosses being made: crosses that stood alone and crosses that decorated other objects and architecture. The second type was meant to compliment or complete a structure, such as the top of a small chapel or a wood cross at the roadside. They could top a stone or granite tombstone, the entrance to a cemetery, or the peak of a shrine. These small crosses were rarely more than twenty-seven inches high and nineteen inches wide with various sizes in between and forged from whatever raw material was available from scraps of material.

Entire crosses made of iron did not make a showing until the 20th century. These stand-alone crosses reached about sixteen feet high (counting the stone base to which they were always secured) and five feet wide. Crosses of such large proportions required special ingot and became something only the wealthy could afford or for which the entire village took up a collection. A cross established at the crossroads before the entrance to the village was meant to prevent the entrance of pestilence, protect against famine, and scare away evil spirits. Many well-to-do people ordered them for the border of a field or the clergy may have ordered four crosses to denote the limits of the parish cemetery.

Iron cross on top of a chapel in Kurzyna Mala, dated 1842.

The earliest iron crosses were simple cruciforms without decoration. With new wealth and the desire to show off that wealth in a visible way and to glorify God with something beautiful, people began ordering crosses with additional decorative touches. The top part of the cross offered the greatest opportunity to introduce intricate work. The places most likely to exhibit decorative ironwork were the very top of the cross, the ends of the arms of the cross, and the center where the arms intersect. The crosses made of metal sometimes had a small roof made of iron or sheet metal to cover the image of Christ crucified. Using a variety of blacksmithing techniques that included forge welding, twisting, and scroll work, the crosses were adorned with leaves, branches, flowers, wavy rays, the sun, the moon, and/or the stars. In the Kurpie region, secular motifs such as a rooster also appear on the crosses. A rooster on a cross was purportedly to remind passers-by of the denial of Jesus by his disciple Simon Peter: "Truly I tell you, this very night, before the cock crows you will deny me." (Matthew 26:33-35). The morning crow of the rooster was also believed to scare away demons of the dark, opening the day to the light, symbolizing Christ. According to some ethnographers, the half moon or crescent moon was in eastern Christian tradition a symbol of the victory of Christianity over paganism which then became a motif in Catholic folk art.

The artists of most roadside shrines remain anonymous but their work endures, standing quietly along a country road as natural to the landscape of Poland as a river or a tree, a lasting legacy cut into wood, chiseled in stone, molded out of clay, painted on canvas, or hammered on an anvil.

CHAPTER 5
Customs
&
Traditions

In the 19th century, Polish ethnographer Oskar Kolberg (1814-1890) conducted field work in every region of Poland and subsequently published a priceless treasure of folk culture in his work of forty-eight volumes titled *LUD* (*The People*). About roadside shrines, he comments: "These objects erected at a crossroads just beyond the village or within it, by religious individuals for the intention of good health, or success in a venture, or as memorials to their departed relatives or for the glory of God, plays an important role in the life of the Polish village."

In building or erecting a cross, chapel, or shrine, the people of Poland created spaces that were distinct from their everyday, worldly places. Always blessed and sanctified by a priest, the shrine became a place made *of* prayer and a place *to* pray and as such, became a sacred place. These small sacred spaces, erected away from a church, were considered to be the most valuable possession of a village or town. They were a public symbol of the villagers' faith but were also much more than that: they anchored them, unified them, and gave them structure and purpose.

A place of prayer, Legionowo, Warsaw region, 2008. Photo credit: Krystyna Bartosik

Prior to building or establishing a shrine, it was customary to ask and receive approval from the local pastor, who may have added his ideas to the entire enterprise as well. It was the local priest who converted a building or statue into a sacred object and sacred space with the blessing of holy water. This dedication or blessing ceremony, during which a new shrine or chapel was unveiled, was a major community event.

In 1910 in Gazeta Olstyńskie, a newspaper correspondent in the Warmia region of northern Poland wrote:

> There was a very lofty celebration on the second day of
> Pentecost. It happened due to the blessing of a new and
> beautiful chapel within which were placed the figures of
> St. Rosalia and that of the Immaculate Conception. The
> chapel was erected through the efforts of the members of the
> community … the celebration took place at 4 pm with the
> pastor the Reverend Kensbok and surrounded by the gathered
> faithful. Earlier "Serdeczna Matko" was sung and after prayers
> to the Holy Ghost, the priest gave a very moving homily
> on following the life and virtues of St. Rosalia and Blessed
> Mother. This was followed by saying the rosary and singing
> "Witaj Krolowo Nieba." The ceremony was concluded by
> sprinkling the edifice or statue with holy water. With uplifted
> hearts, everyone returned to their homes.

The shrine usually occupied one of the most important locations in the town or village. Oftentimes fenced in, it marked off sacred ground (*sacrum*) from the worldly (*profane*) road, trod by mere mortals. It is not a coincidence that the shrines are often surrounded by trees. It was customary to erect the shrine near an existing tree or to plant two or more trees nearby—linden, ash, oak, pine or sycamore. Frequently chosen was the linden tree, a tree dedicated to the Blessed Virgin Mary and felt to bring good fortune. By the second half of the 19th century, a pair of evergreen arborvitae (*Thuja occidentalis*) called *żywotnik*, was often typically planted. Also popular was the hardy *Rosa rugosa*, varieties of lilacs, and perennial and annual flowers that would adorn the shrine through the summer months.

Whether erected on the initiation of a private individual or family, or the entire community, the shrine was everyone's responsibility. Each village, town, or city that could claim a shrine or chapel assumed responsibility for its maintenance and upkeep.

In 1994, during the renovation of one of the small wooden shrines attached to a tree near Kraków, a letter was found tucked under the roof. The note read: "We erected this little wayside shrine for the glory of the Blessed Virgin Mary in hopes that she will come to our aid at the time of our death … if someone should remove the roof of this shrine and reads this letter, please pray for those of us who erected this shrine and may you refurbish it and make it new for the continued glory of the Most Blessed Mary." It was signed "Your friends in life and death." Those who found the letter did as instructed and when replacing the shrine, added their own letter to that of the original one for the next generation to heed: "In the next few decades, when perhaps we are no longer here, may someone take care of and repair this wonderful shrine where children, passer-by and travelers can stop to praise the glory of the Blessed Virgin Mary."

That a roadside shrine beyond repair had to be replaced in the same spot is documented over and over again by Polish ethnographers conducting interviews and research on roadside shrines. When a wooden shrine or cross began to show signs of wear and tear, it was repaired, never just randomly torn down and discarded or burned. If the wooden shrine was completely ruined and beyond salvation, then the old wood would be burned as the fire of the Easter Vigil on Holy Saturday near the church or at a special bonfire on the feast day of the saint to which the shrine was dedicated. Another such time is mentioned by Zygmunt Gloger, author of *Encyklopedia Staropolska* who wrote: "It was the universal custom at one time to have a meal at home after visiting the graves of the dead on the feast of All Souls (November 2). Afterwards everyone who had gathered together would go to the local wooden crosses for the purpose of repairing or providing supports for those that were leaning or if the base was entirely rotted, to dig them out, cut out the rotten part and replace it again in the same spot."

If a wooden cross was rotted where it met the ground, it was cut and buried again and could hold up for another twenty years or more. Since some of the original crosses were thirty-two feet tall, this could be done quite a few times. The reason for the cross being placed there may long have been forgotten but because it had been placed there and had been blessed, it was considered holy ground. Its placement by newer generations continued to be respected and maintained in the same spot. If a tree holding a small chapel on its trunk happened to be blown down or if it rotted away, the shrine was fastened to a post or placed within a niche on a pillar in the same spot. The tree itself was also considered sacred and when land and forests were cleared, the tree hosting a shrine was never cut down. Even if the tree was withered and dying it was left untouched. Strong was the belief that anyone who took an axe or saw to such a tree would meet with grave misfortune.

This same belief was also true of taking apart a brick structure or shrine as exemplified by this story from Warmia in the 1870s:

> On the grounds of a landowner named Hermann there was a brick chapel dedicated to the Blessed Mother. The chapel was in his way in the field and with the approval of the pastor, he took it apart and used the bricks to build a stable. The figure of the Blessed Mother with a crown, the pastor hid in the attic of the rectory. According to statements made by locals Hermann got sick with an incurable disease and the horses in the stable died off. At the same time the pastor sickened with ulcers and he then ascertained that it was heavenly punishment for taking apart the chapel. He instructed that a new one be built in another place between two beautiful linden trees in which was placed the figure of the Blessed Mother from the old chapel. When close to death, the pastor made it known that his grave was to be located close to the entrance of the new chapel, so that the people would walk over his grave as punishment for his sin towards the Blessed Mother.

Another important aspect of maintaining a cross, chapel, or figure of a saint was decorating it and keeping it looking beautiful. Generally, this was the work of women who lived nearby and dedicated themselves to maintaining the shrine and considered it to be sacred work, very often a responsibility that was passed on to daughters and granddaughters.

Cleaning a shrine usually began a few days before Easter by removing old flowers and wreaths and then decorating throughout the rest of the year. For holy days, the shrines and crosses would be festooned with branches of oak or wreaths of periwinkle (*Vinca minor*). During the spring or summer months, fresh flowers from the garden and meadows were, and still are, used to decorate the shrines. When fresh flowers were unavailable, the women of Poland used tissue and crepe paper to make "flowers" into bouquets and garlands, and sometimes mixed them with the green branches of pine, spruce, or some other shrub to adorn the shrine. In recent years, silk and plastic

Illustration of decorating of a roadside shrine, date unknown.
Photo credit: Panstwowe Muzeum Etnograficzne w Warszawie

flowers have replaced tissue paper but continue to please the eye and gladden the heart nonetheless. The color of the paper flowers used in decoration was important. For instance, for the figures of Christ and martyred saints, the preferred color was red, symbolizing suffering. For figures of the Blessed Mother, tradition dictates that the colors be blue or white, the symbol of purity. For St. Joseph, orange and yellow lilies or flowers were preferred.

The shrines and chapels were maintained on a daily basis, but special attention and decoration was showered on them during the religious holiday associated with the represented figures. For instance, in April or early May, any statue devoted to the Blessed Virgin Mary was cleaned and decorated in preparation for the month of May which is dedicated to the Blessed Virgin Mary.

"Today the village girls have brought to the altar of the Virgin Mother the first tribute of spring—fresh sheaves of greenery; everything was decked with nosegays and garlands – the altar, the image, and even the belfry and the galleries. Sometimes a morning zephyr, stirring from the east, would tear down the garlands and throw them upon the kneeling worshippers, and would spread fragrance abroad as from a priest's censer."
—Adam Mickiewicz, *Pan Tadeusz*, Book XI

Prior to March 19th any figure of St. Joseph would receive special attention in preparation for the Feast of St. Joseph. The same would be done for the feast of St. John the Baptist prior to June 24th. June was also dedicated to the Sacred Heart of Jesus and any images of the Sacred Heart would be the focus of attention and freshening up before June.

FEAST DAYS

Each community had their favored saints and shrines and paid special homage to them. On the feast day of that particular saint, the villagers would gather together to pray a specific litany and sing religious songs. If the village or town could boast a church, the congregation would process from the church to the statue and conduct a special service there. In centuries past churches were not as numerous as today. Small villages often lacked their own church and the faithful had to travel many miles, either on foot or by wagon, to attend church. If that was the case, the faithful gathered instead at the nearest shrine to pray together and conduct a religious service there. The small chapels built like miniature churches often functioned

Illustration titled "Bagpiper in the village" by Antoni Kozakiewicz, 1879.
Photo credit: Panstwowe Muzeum Etnograficzne w Warszawie

for this purpose but even a shrine of a saint, blessed by the church, provided a place to gather, share the faith, and socialize.

HOLY WEEK AND HOLY SATURDAY

In some villages in Poland one form of worship during Holy Week was to decorate the local cross with flowers and greenery and to

Blessing of baskets on Holy Saturday, Worochota, now Ukraine, 1933. Photo credit: Narodowe Archiwum Cyfrowe

Gathering at shrine for blessing of baskets on Holy Saturday, Grębałów, locality in Kraków, 2021. Photo credit: Gregorsz Graff

burn candles before it. In the Poznań region this custom occurred throughout Lent. In the Mazowsze region, one of the customs on Holy Saturday had been to gather at the cross and sing religious hymns all night into Easter Sunday. This custom of gathering under the cross and singing also took place the following weeks (Saturdays into Sundays) right up until Pentecost Sunday—the entire Eastertide period.

The blessing of food on Holy Saturday is an ancient Polish tradition. A basket or bowl was filled with hardboiled eggs, cheese, sausage and/or ham, bread, horseradish, and whatever else the good housewife had prepared. This food was blessed by a priest on Holy Saturday and called *swięconka*, meaning "blessed." The contents were consumed on Easter Sunday morning after the Resurrection mass. It was the custom in some regions for the priest to go from home to home via horse and wagon blessing each parishioner's food. Sometimes it was customary for one of the homes in the village to be chosen as the gathering place for the blessing of the baskets and everyone would assemble there to await the priest. In regions where there was only one parish for numerous small villages and hamlets, the designated spot for the blessing of food was a roadside shrine at a crossroads. Mothers and children would walk or ride to the shrine clutching their baskets, anxious not to miss the priest. This custom had a resurgence during the Covid-19 pandemic as evidenced by the photo on opposite page taken in Grębałów, at one time a village outside Kraków, but now incorporated into the city.

ROGATION DAYS *DNI KRZYŻOWE*

From the time of the Middle Ages, down through the centuries and even today in some regions of Poland, peasants held processions called *krzyżowników* or *dni kryżowe*, meaning cross bearer or days of the cross. This was a day where the community marched around the fields carrying crosses (hence the name) and banners, singing religious songs, and processing to any cross in the nearby vicinity. This procession is also known as the Blessing of the Fields. In the 15th century, the dates for the processions and blessings of the fields were determined by the church. Also called *dies rogationum* (Rogation Days, or days of supplication), the name is related to the pleading nature of the solemn prayers inspired by the Gospel of John:16-23. "I tell you the truth: the Father will give you whatever you ask of Him in my name." They take place on the Monday, Tuesday, and Wednesday

ST. ISIDORE THE PLOWMAN

Often invoked in prayer during the Rogation Days is St. Isidore the Plowman (*Św. Izydor Oracz*), whose feast day (May 15th) runs close to these particular days but mostly because he is the patron saint of farmers in Poland. Born in poverty in Spain, Isidore as a young man had to work as a farmhand for his wealthy neighbor. He tilled, plowed, and sowed by the sweat of his brow. An extremely hard worker, Isidore was also extremely devout, always combin-

Illustration of St. Isidore the Plowman. Photo credit: Wikimedia.

ing his work with prayer. As a role model, he elevated working the land to that of a blessing, which found numerous followers not just in Poland but in agrarian countries throughout Europe. He became a model for Christian farmers. Banners with images of this saint or his figure on a portable bier were often carried through the fields. This Spanish saint, promoted through the Jesuits at the beginning in the 17th century, can be seen in church paintings, as a figure in roadside shrines, or woodcuts or illustrations on the walls of small roadside chapels. In paintings, he is depicted as a man kneeling in prayer, sometimes with a staff, and two angels behind a plow tilling the fields. On his actual feast day, this patron saint of farmers is honored with a special mass for the intention of farmers and a good harvest.

Shrine dedicated to St. Isidore dated 1863, Kornatka, Myślenic County. Photo credit: Michał Zalewski

Gathering at shrine to begin procession for Blessing of the Fields on Rogation Day, 1993.

before Ascension Thursday. On Monday the prayers focus on a good harvest. On Tuesday they are for the sanctification of human labor; and on the third day, for the hungry. They also take place on the feast of St. Mark on April 25.

The procession during Rogation Days takes place after Mass. The priest stands at the foot of the steps leading to the altar and begins with a prayer for the reversal of all types of misfortune and calamities. "Let us pray to God the Father Almighty that he may cleanse the earth of all mistakes, repel illness, return the wandering and heal the sick." This is followed by the Litany to All Saints during which time everyone kneels until the invocation of the Blessed Virgin Mary at which time everyone stands. When St. Peter is invoked, the entire congregation begins to move outdoors while continuing to sing the litany. In some parishes, the faithful gather at a shrine. The procession, with the priest at its head, processes through footpaths along the fields praying for successful crops, often stopping at all wayside shrines and especially at any crosses. The fields are blessed by the priest. At some selected corners of the field shrines, the verses of the gospel are buried. The priest and parishioners process to another church if there is one nearby or head to a field or road towards a wayside shrine or cross. There the priest says more prayers for good

Burying the gospel at one of the boundaries of the field, 1993.

weather and rain. The procession returns to church, again singing a litany or favored songs, most often "*Boże w dobroci*" ("God in His Goodness") or "*Kto się w opiece odda Panu swemu*" ("He who places himself in the care of the Lord"). On returning to the church, the congregation prays Psalm 69 ("Save me, O God") and the concluding prayers associated with the litany to all the saints.

THE MAY DEVOTIONS
NABOŻEŃSTWA MAJOWE/MAJÓWKI

Majówki is an affectionate term used by the people of Poland for the devotion services held in churches, at grottos, chapels, and roadside figures in the evenings throughout the month of May. These May vespers to the Blessed Virgin Mary began in Spain and spread quickly throughout Europe through the efforts of the Jesuits. In Poland, the first May devotion was held in Warsaw at Holy Cross (*Św. Krzyża*) Church in 1852 and was quickly adopted by all of Poland. Traditionally, on May 1, a special Mass dedicated to the Blessed Virgin Mary was held in churches. After the mass the entire congregation, led by the priest, processed to the nearest Marian shrine where

Faithful praying at shrine dedicated to Blessed Virgin Mary, Ruda, Stalowa Wola County. Photo credit: Jadwiga and Krzysztof Stańczyk 2008

with songs, prayer, and complete adoration, she was crowned with a circle of flowers as Queen of Heaven and Queen of Poland.

In villages located some distance from a church, the special service to Mary was held outside at roadside shrines with her image, or at a cross if that was the only local roadside shrine. In preparation for the May devotions, the shrine or chapel was freshened and decorated with spring flowers (lilacs and tulips and tree blossoms) and with the leaves of trees such as oak.

The *majówki* took place in the evening, between 7 p.m. (less often 6 p.m.) and 8 p.m., after work in the field or on the farm was finished, and when the house and barnyard had been settled for the day. Throughout the month of May, men, women, and children would gather at the shrine to pray the rosary, say the Litany of Loreto, called *Litania Loretanska* in Polish, and sing much loved religious songs dedicated to the Blessed Virgin Mary, such as "*Cześć Maryi, Chwalcie łąki umajone*," or "*Po górach dolinach.*" If there was a chapel with an

Prayers at a cross containing a small shrine of the Blessed Virgin Mary at base, 2008, Kruzyna Mała, Nisko County.
Photo credit: Jadwiga and Krzysztof Stańczyk

altar inside, candles would be lit during the service. Families would take turns making sure there were some fresh flowers on the altar or at the base of the figure.

If there were benches, and in some instances, kneelers, those who felt inclined would remain to pray for special intentions after the others had gone. Sometimes the faithful would carry kerosene lamps to the service in order to light their way home if they stayed to sing and pray long after sunset. In the instances of inclement weather, the service was moved indoors at someone's house in front of the home altar.

Author Władysław Reymont captured the May service in honor of the Mother of God in in the Łowicz region in his work *The Peasants* in the 1925 volume dedicated to spring:

> *"... close to the lich-gate, there stood a little shrine containing a statue of the mother of God. Every May, the girls adorned it with paper ribbons and a gilt crown, and cast wild flowers all around, doing likewise all they could to preserve it from complete ruin. It was of great antiquity, and so cracked and*

crumbling and dilapidated that the birds no longer made their nests in it; and if a shepherd-boy ever took shelter there, it was only during the autumn rains. To some extent it was screened from the winter storms by the churchyard trees, the old lindens, the slender birches, and a few crosses which stood near, leaning out of the perpendicular. [...] The blacksmith knelt at the front, at foot of the figure, sprinkled with tulips and rose hawthorn, and struck up a hymn [...] And the people looked into their Mother's face, and lifted their voices, while she stretched her hands out in benediction over the world.

"Good night, O Lily White! Good night! Mary, our hearts' delight, Good night!"

Also popular were rosary devotions to the Blessed Virgin Mary in the month of October, something that was adopted in Polish churches later than the May devotions. The growth of the October rosary devotions was decided on October 1, 1883, by decree of Pope Leon XIII, who resolved that October would be dedicated to Our Lady of the Rosary. From that time on, with edicts and encouragements from local bishops and diocese, October became another month when the people of Poland would gather at the shrines and chapels to pray the rosary.

LEŻAJSK'S APPARITIONS

The roadside shrines were not limited to special functions just on high holy days but were deeply engrained in all aspects of daily life. Oftentimes, when the smallest hamlet or village did not have a church of its own, the first holy space to be established was a cross, a shrine of a saint or the Blessed Virgin Mary, or a small chapel that would act as a very small church. In the *Kalendarz Katolicki Krakowski* from 1886 we read about just such a beginning in the town of Leżajsk in southeastern Poland: "… it hosts a painting of the Blessed Virgin Mother that is credited with numerous miracles. Here in 1590, the Blessed Virgin Mary with the Infant and St. Joseph appeared to Tomasz Michałek. She asked that he erect a church at the site. Immediately they built a little chapel, then a wooden church and in 1606 invited the Bernardines to settle here." Today the site hosts a magnificent church dedicated to the Blessed Virgin Mary, and a Bernardine monastery.

Shrine dedicated to the Sacred Heart of
Jesus with inset showing a close-up of the
statue, Okrągłe, Tarnobrzeg region. The
inscription reads: "Lord Jesus, bless us."

JUNE DEVOTIONS TO THE SACRED HEART *NABOŻEŃSTWO CZERWCOWE*

The roadside chapels and shrines were also the site of *Nabożeństwo Czerwcowe,* also called the *czerwcówki* — the June devotions to the Sacred Heart of Jesus. It was French Roman Catholic nun Marie Margaret Alacoque who promoted devotion to the Sacred Heart of Jesus as Catholics know it today. She had visions of Jesus Christ that revealed to her the form that devotions should take including First Friday devotions and Eucharistic adoration.

The Feast of the Sacred Heart was established by the church to take place in June. In Poland, devotion to the Sacred Heart of Jesus was first said at the church of the Nuns of the Visitation (the order to which Margaret Mary Alacoque belonged) in Lublin on June 1, 1857 and readily taken up by the diocese. After official sanction by Pope Pius IX in 1873, the devotion to the Sacred Heart of Jesus spread throughout Poland.

The June service consists of adoration of the Blessed Sacrament and the Litany of the Sacred Heart of Jesus. While devotions took place inside churches, they also took place at roadside shrines and chapels and especially at crosses. The faithful gathered during the evening during the month of June to recite the Litany to the Sacred Heart and sing religious songs dedicated to the Sacred Heart.

THE FEAST OF CORPUS CHRISTI

The feast of Corpus Christi, *Boże Ciało* in Polish, the day on which the Catholic Church commemorates the institution of the Holy Eucharist, is one of the greatest Christian holy days. The feast day is marked by eucharistic processions, during which the Blessed Sacrament is carried in a monstrance through the church and into the streets. In Poland it is celebrated with tremendous joy in the form of masses and processions that lead to four different altars. These altars could be erected in small tents or pavilion-like structures made of cloth and adorned with holy pictures and statues, or if the town or village could boast such, the procession would visit four different shrines—be it a cross, a figure on a pedestal, or a small chapel.

In the large cities of Poland, the Corpus Christi procession is led by bishops and clergy in richly embroidered and decorated vestments followed by all the monks and religious houses and accompanied by

One of four altars of Corpus Christi procession, 1993, Kadzidło, Ostrołęka County.

trumpets and drums. In smaller towns and villages, it is done with less ostentation but certainly with equal fervor. Dressed with pride in full regional costumes, the faithful processes to whatever shrine is within the town limits and any additional altars that had to be erected. There the Blessed Sacrament rests while the assembled kneel to pray, sing, and listen to readings from the four evangelists—Matthew, Mark, Luke, and John—regarding the Eucharist. The procession then continues in the same manner to the other shrines and altars.

THE AVE-BELLS *(SYGNATURKA)*
AND THE ANGELUS

The small chapels were often built with a tower and bell, much like a big, established church. The smallest of the church bells in an established church was called the *sygnaturka*, and so the small bell placed on the top of a roadside chapel was also called a *sygnaturka*. Both were known as an ave-bell. This bell organized not only religious life within a community, but it was also a mode of communication and sharing of information and gave structure to village life on a day-to-day basis.

One of the most important roles of the ave-bell was to announce the Angelus at 6 am, 12 noon, and 6 pm, instructing the people to pray the Angelus wherever they stood, be it the orchard, farmhouse, or field. The Angelus is a short practice of devotion in honor of the Incarnation, a word used to express the idea of Jesus Christ coming to earth in human form. The Angelus, Latin for "angel," comes from the first few words of the text *Angelus Domini nuntiavit Maria* ("The Angel of the Lord declared unto Mary"). The angel referred to in the text is Gabriel, a messenger of God who revealed to the Virgin Mary that she would conceive a child to be born the Son of God (Luke 1:26–38), which is known as the Annunciation. That event is contained in the words of the Hail Mary prayer.

Most people associate the Angelus with a noontime prayer, but it first appeared as a single evening prayer among the Franciscans in Italy because that was the hour in which the angel was to have appeared to Mary. This saying of three Hail Marys in the evening was announced by the ringing of a bell. In 1327, Pope John XXII approved the ringing of evening bells throughout Rome to signal the praying of three Hail Marys (which are also called "Aves," hence the name ave-bell). The Angelus developed into its distinctive ringing three times a day over a period of centuries. Most historical sources agree that it was patterned after the daily prayer in the medieval monasteries — today known as the Liturgy of the Hours, with morning, noon, and evening prayer.

The pattern of the ave-bells for the Angelus was three rings, a pause, three rings, a pause, three rings. In some parishes in Poland this was followed by an additional nine rings in succession that would call the people of Poland to pray for those who had died in battle. The ringing of the bell gave pause amidst the hustle of everyday life

Painting called "The Angelus" by Aleksander Gierymski, 1890.
Photo credit: Muzeum Narodowe w Waszawie

to stop and give devotion. "The sun had gone down, the earth was bathed in the after glow, as with a golden dew. All was still; all things held their peace, listening as it were to the sounds of the Angelus; everything seemed in unison—a prayer of quietude and thanksgiving for the blessing of the day that was over ..." wrote author Władyław Reymont in his book *The Peasants*, recalling the evening bell in the small village of Lipka.

In the days where clocks and watches were rare, the ave-bell became the signal for the villagers to gather at the chapel to start out for the church and mass that was located a few miles away. The faithful formed a procession walking from the chapel or shrine towards the church, singing religious songs along the road until they reached their destination. The bell was also rung when pilgrims were passing through the village on their way to a holy place. The villagers would meet them at the village shrine or chapel, pray there together, oftentimes walking with them to the boundaries of their village and sometimes joining them in the pilgrimage towards their destination.

If the bell rang at other times, it informed the villagers that the priest was on his way to someone very sick and called for those listening to pray for a dying individual. It was again rung to notify everyone of the death and acted as another call for prayers for the departed soul. For the next three days while the departed was laid out at home, the community was to say an "Eternal rest" after the Angelus prayers on behalf of the deceased.

The *sygnaturka* fulfilled secular as well as sacred functions. It called the villagers to gather together in the event of a fire, flood, or some other calamity that may have occurred. The bell was rung in a particular way that told the villagers what was happening. Everyone knew the meaning of the bell based on the type of ring, frequency, etc. A person was usually appointed to attend to the ringing and was paid a small stipend or received goods in exchange. In the Warmia region, the bells were often taken care of by women. They had to attend classes to learn the various special ringing of the bells that signaled various happenings in the village. This honorable work was often passed down from mother to daughter.

BELLS OF LORETO

Mentioned here, also, should be the bells and bell towers called the bells of Loreto known in Poland as *dzwonnice Loretanskie*. The history of these bells in Poland began in Italy in the hill town of Loreto. The main attraction there is the Basilica della Santa Casa, a church that was built around the holy house that is believed to be the home in which the Virgin Mary raised Jesus. The holy house is thought to have been brought from Nazareth to Loreto, via Croatia, in 1294. According to legend, the house was borne through the air by angels but an alternative explanation is that crusaders moved the house to Italy brick by brick. In 1469 the Basilica della

Free standing tower with a Loreto bell, 1928, Żywiec County.
Photo credit: Narodowe Archiwum Cyfrowe

Santa Casa was built around the small, holy house, and in 1510 the Church approved Loreto as a Marian shrine and an official place of pilgrimage. Between 1750 and 1754 a large bell tower designed by the Italian architect Luigi Vanvitelli was built next to the basilica, and miniature Loreto hand bells became popular religious souvenirs brought back to the home country of the pilgrims. What made the bells special was that they were bought during a pilgrimage to the sanctuary of Loreto in Italy and believed to have protective qualities. An ancient and lingering belief for many centuries was that the sound of bells had magic in it, including the driving away of evil spirits as far away as the sound of the bell could be heard. Included in that list of evil spirits were those that brought on dark clouds that led to hail or lightning or storms that had the power to destroy crops. When dark clouds began forming, portending the possibility of a calamity, these handbells were rung to drive away the storm. In his *Pamiętnik czasów moich* (*Memoir of My Times*) published posthumously in 1848, Julian Ursyn Niemcewicz (1758-1841) wrote: "When a storm arose and lightning was flashing my mother gave me a small bell from Loreto and in spite of the downpour told me to walk around the house and ring the bell; the clergy told her that ringing the bell would protect the home and everyone in it."

In addition to the small handbells, attaching large bells to existing chapels became popular in parts of Poland. They could also be erected in a free-standing tower. The bells did not have to come from Loreto per se, but be blessed and dedicated to Our Lady of Loreto. With time, the Loreto bell also came to be used as a *sygnaturka*, the ave-bell, to remind people to say the Angelus prayer and call the faithful for the daily May and rosary services.

Loreto bell attached to a chapel devoted to St. Valentine erected in 1811, Targowisko, Wieliczka County.
Photo credit: Krzysztof Urbański

BEGGARS *DZIADY*

The city streets and country roads of Poland were rife with all the holy picture sellers, traveling troupes, and pilgrims. Among those on the road were also beggars, the *dziady*. They could be seen at funerals, at the cemetery on All Souls Day, at the innumerable church feast days throughout the country, and often traveling long distances to holy places throughout the country. Unlike in the West, where being a beggar was considered shameful, beggars in Poland fulfilled an important role in the community and had certain recognized functions and claims to dignity. They provided prayers and religious songs to elevate the soul. The giver of alms received credit in heaven by giving to the poor beggar in need.

Chapel with beggar resting in front, 1942 (no location noted).
Photo credit: Narodowe Archiwum Cyfrowe

Along the roads and path more frequently used, beggars traveling the roads would stop and rest at a cross or figure. Oftentimes he or she could find sanctuary in a small chapel during a storm or protection from the burning heat of an open road on a summer's day. With no real place to live, they sometimes settled in for a while to sing from the Psalms and Book of Canticles, calling on people to give them alms. Up until the 19th century it also wasn't uncommon for a hermit to pull together a makeshift shanty against the wall of a chapel located deep in a wood and live there in solitude and prayer.

"Peasant girl before a shrine" by artist Antoni Kozakiewicz, 1894.
Photo credit: Muzeum Narodowe w Warszawie

ROADSIDE SHRINES IN EVERYDAY LIFE

A village shrine or chapel served as the heart of the community. In Reymont's novel titled *The Peasants: Summer,* one of the characters says "Where are we to meet?" The response is "At the crucifix by the forest, where we are going at once." The line highlights how a village cross, shrine, or small chapel was used as a meeting place where people gathered for whatever reason: to hold councils or deliberations on a Sunday; to say a private prayer while passing by; to pray during misfortune; where a young man would walk a sweetheart home from evening devotions in May; where a young couple pledged their troth to each other in secret before the official sanction from their parents; where feuding neighbors vowed to reconcile their differences; where lost items were left to be reclaimed by the rightful owner; where people would bury their money during times of war and uncertainty; where guns were buried during the numerous Polish insurrections against Austria, Russia, and Prussia; where secret messages were left by the insurrectionists prior to the January Uprising of 1863. It was also a place where those who committed suicide, those who died as part of mass murders—anyone who left this world without receiving the sacraments—would be buried. The shrine or chapel made the space holy, providing the deceased with some measure of peace as well as protection to the living from wandering souls looking for absolution.

In those earlier centuries, the chapels and shrines across the country often acted as a road map, frequently followed by those on the road to somewhere. At a time when roads were poorly marked, if at all, the chapels, statues, and crosses were used as signposts to provide directions to a stranger or pilgrim or to make decisions along the road. One would be advised to "make a left at the shrine of St. Florian," or "when you get to St. Onufry, turn right and the path will take you to the forester's cottage," or "we'll stop and feed the horses at St. Stanislaus."

For travelers and especially for pilgrims, a roadside shrine or chapel was often a rest stop, a place to meditate, to say the rosary, or sing hymns as a way of preparing themselves to arrive at their special sanctuary or destination. The shrines, often located under the shade of a tree, offered respite from heat. A bench welcomed them as a place to rest. Some shrines were located next to streams or lakes which provided water to quench thirst or to soak dusty, weary feet. It may also have provided a beautiful view that uplifted the heart, providing a spiritual as well as a physical resting place. In addition, if a town or village contained a special sanctuary or was celebrating a particular feast day that attracted the pilgrims to travel to their town, the pilgrims were often greeted by the townspeople at the first shrine on entering the town as a sign of welcome. When the pilgrims left, they were accompanied by the townspeople or villagers to the last shrine outside their town limits, to direct them further on.

The shrines and chapels often marked the beginning and end of

Postcard from a painting by Adam Setkowicz titled "Our Father
…" Photo credit: private collection of Krystyna Bartosik

town or village boundaries and where paths led into a forest as a short cut to another village. When the roads were covered with a high layer of snow, the shrines facilitated orientation to the landscape. They often appeared on legal documents, indicating property boundaries, or on historical maps denoting the founding of a new parish.

If someone was leaving for the bigger world, such as soldiers going off to war, a son or daughter emigrating to America, or a pilgrim going to some holy place, the village shrine or cross was where they said goodbye to their home and families and asked for blessings for their journey and endeavors. If someone was leaving and not returning for a long time, sometimes the entire village would walk them to the outskirts of the village to the shrine where they would say their farewells. Someone who had been gone a long time would also stop on their way into the village to pray and give thanks for their safe return. Greetings were also exchanged here by someone who was returning after a long absence especially anyone who was considered a criminal. Before crossing over into the village boundaries, the in-

OATH OF BROTHERHOOD

This painting by Juliusz Kossak called "Oath of Brotherhood," painted in 1857, depicts an old Polish custom of swearing fraternal love before a roadside shrine. As the title indicates this swearing of fraternal love was a vow, an oath of brotherhood (*Bracia ślubne*) that was faithfully kept to the grave. This brotherhood, this commitment to each other, can be understood by men who have experienced military combat together no matter the country or century. The words of Zygmunt Kaczkowski, Polish writer and independence activist sums up this fraternity beautifully: "And when we have one penny, then half will belong to one, and half to the other. And if we both have only one hand left, then this hand is to work for both of us. And if we both have only two legs left, then those legs are to bear the bodies of both."

Photo credit: Wikimedia

Postcard from a painting titled "Powrót do Ojczyzny" ("Return to Homeland") by Adam Setkowicz, 1912.
Photo credit: Wikipedia

dividual had to stop here and reconcile with God and his fellow man before entering the village. Day-to-day, walking past a shrine, cross, or chapel on the way to market or to visit a neighbor, the faithful would remove their hats and/or bow their head towards the shrine, make the sign of the cross, or stop and kneel to say a prayer. One prayer often said when passing a cross was: "*Kłaniamy się Tobie Chryste, i błogosławimy Ciebie, żeś krzyż swój świat odkupić raczył*" ("We bow to you Jesus Christ and bless you, that through your cross you have redeemed the world"). Another short prayer was: "*Któryś cierpiał za nas rany, Jezu Chryste, zmiłuje się nad nami*" ("You who suffered for us Jesus Christ, have mercy on us").

It was inevitable that the shrines even became incorporated into proverbs and sayings such as: "*Modli się pod figurą, a nosi diabła za skórą*" ("Prays beneath the figure but carries the devil under his skin") and "*Ucieka jak złe od krzyża*" ("Ran away like evil from a cross").

The shrines were so central to the landscape, so important in the lives of individuals, that they influenced every sphere of the arts. They were the subject of literature by some of Poland's most famous writers and poets, such as Adam Mickiewicz's *Powrót Taty* (*Father's Return*), a poem for children, whose opening lines

Postcard by artist Z. Skawinski, 1915.

embody the role of a roadside shrine in day-to-day worries and troubles:

"Run, all of you, beyond the village, to the shrine on the hill.
Your father has not returned these mornings and nights
and with tears I worry and await his return.
The rivers are flooded, animals roam the forests
and the roads filled with wandering brigands."

Hearing this, the children run to the statue on the hill
and begin their prayers.
They kiss the ground, then: "In the name of the Father,
The Son and the Holy Spirit,
Be praised, Most Holy Trinity,
Now and forever."
Then: "Our Father" "Hail Mary"… and "I Believe"
a decade said, and then the entire rosary.
When they finished, their prayer books from their pockets they pulled

Spirit of Place

And sing the Litany, "Have mercy, have mercy, dear Mother,
on our dear father…"

When they hear the sound of wheels on the road…"

(Author translation)

Other poets and writers who also wrote about the village shrines include Stanisław Balinski, Jan Kasprowicz, Emil Lentarowicz, and Cyprian Kamil Norwid. This poem is by Stanisław Balinski:

How hard our land's peculiar charm to tell:

Its amber fields, its rosy hawthorn, and the breeze

That sings its way through starlit pines; the spell

Of crosses by the wayside, rowan shrubs, primeval trees.

No less influenced were those who expressed their art in painting, including Vlastimil Hofman, Julian Fałat, Stanisław Czajkowski, and Józef Chełmonski to name just a few.

And at the very end, at death, the roadside shrine was a final stopping place before burial. Carried out of church after the funeral mass,

Painting by Vlastimil Hofman titled "Confession," 1906.
Photo credit: Muzeum Narodowe w Warszawie

Customs and Traditions

the body was transported to the cemetery by the gathered congregation, who formed a procession. Even as late as the 1980s this was often done on foot, the casket carried by horse and carriage. As the funeral procession arrived at the shrine or cross leading out of the village to the cemetery, it stopped for the *odpraszanie* or *przemowa pożegalna*, the forgiveness speech and final goodbye. Here, at the shrine that had played such a critical role in his or her everyday life, the deceased, through an individual speaking for him/her, asked for forgiveness from his community of any transgressions or any hurts caused during his/her lifetime. In this last communication with his family and community, forgiveness was granted and prayers were said for his/her everlasting soul. There were even those individuals who erected a cross at the roadside during their lifetime with the request that after their death their remains stop at the cross before burial. The *dziady*, the beggar, would be there waiting, his prayers and lamentations louder than those of the mourners and viewed as fitting and right.

* * *

On a community level, the presence or the establishment of a shrine serves as historian to the desires of all the members of a community who may have contributed to its existence. On an individual and personal level, the shrines provided order and structure in a world that could be chaotic and unpredictable. They offered protection and safety against evil and dangerous elements, organized villagers' lives throughout the year with expected behaviors, created opportunities for socialization, generated community solidarity, and most importantly, allowed for and provided opportunities for the people to express their sorrows, joys, and needs.

The roadside shrines of Poland are more than just beautiful structures in the landscape. They deeply reflect the country's history and politics, its artists, its customs and traditions. They are evidence of the hopes, sorrows, and joys of the Polish people. They are the visible manifestation of the faith, prayers, and history of a nation and encapsulate the spirit of Poland down through the centuries.

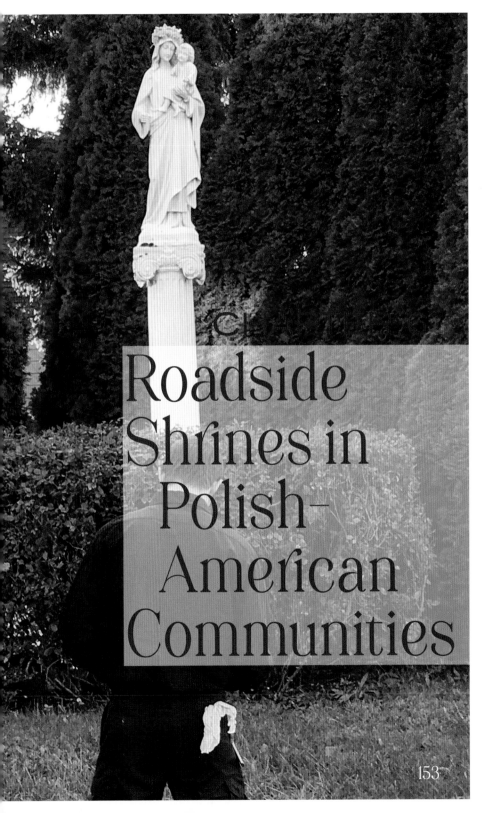

Roadside Shrines in Polish-American Communities

During the 19th and 20th centuries, massive numbers of Poles left the country of their birth and immigrated to America. The early immigrants of the middle 1800s settled down in the rural areas of Texas and Wisconsin. One of the regions that saw the establishment of roadside shrines was Portage County in central Wisconsin where Poles established large settlements in the 1860s and also constructed numerous roadside shrines on their properties. Conducting field research in the late 1980s, Dennis Kolinski, a Polish-American ethnographer who had studied wayside crosses in Poland, was able to document the presence of over fifty wayside shrines in this predominantly rural central Wisconsin region and commented that "the crosses and shrines found in central Wisconsin exhibit almost the same degree of variety in function and form as their precursors from the Polish village." Existing crosses were in-

scribed with dates of 1911 and 1935 but estimates of the age of the others went back to 1875. The motivations for erecting shrines and crosses were varied. Some wanted to have the landscape look like that of their village in Poland. Others recalled hearing of how a crossroad was haunted—strange creatures or "devils" would appear and disappear on a particular corner and so a cross was erected there.

Other regions, which had a few wayside shrines or crosses but not as prolific as Portage County were the Polish American settlements near Pulaski, Wisconsin, and in Warsaw, North Dakota. Another rural region that took up the custom in larger numbers were the Polish immigrants to Wilno, in northern Ontario, Canada. The early

This roadside shrine in Wilno, Canada, was restored and rededicated in 2005 when on the brink of being lost.
Photo credit: Wilno Heritage Society

Shrine dedicated to Our Lady of Częstochowa, Wilno, North Ontario, Canada, 2012. Photo credit: Andrew Golebiowski

settlers who arrived in this part of the remote area of Renfrew County experienced great difficulties along poor roads and long distances getting to the nearest church to attend services. Like their ancestors did in Poland, the immigrants erected crosses and shrines at various crossroads where they could gather together to pray and recite the rosary until they could build their own church, which they did in 1875. The community continues to cherish and maintain these structures and it has become a popular place for visitors from both Canada and the United States. With these few exceptions, the presence of large numbers of roadside shrines within rural Polish American communities or Polish immigrant communities in other parts of the world, has not been preserved, has been lost with the passage of time, did not develop extensively, or was just not studied and documented.

Undated home altar in Baltimore, MD. Photo credit: *Elinor Cahn.*
East Baltimore Documentary Photography Project Collection, The Photography
Collections, University of Maryland, Baltimore County

In the massive immigration to America that took place at the
turn of the 20th century "for bread" the Poles settled chiefly in industrial cities of the Northeast and Midwest where they could easily
find jobs and carve themselves a piece of the American dream. They
banded together in closely knit communities, and the life of most
Polish Americans continued, as it did in Poland, to revolve around
the liturgical calendar of the church. They held May processions to
the Blessed Mother in May, took their baskets to be blessed on Holy
Saturday, never held weddings during Lent or Advent, fasted as required, gave their children up to God as priests and nuns, and built
astonishingly beautiful churches in which to worship and practice
their faith.

Given the vital role the roadside shrines played in village life in
Poland, it would seem natural and expected that the custom of erect-

ing roadside shrines everywhere would have transferred to the new country. The earlier generation of immigrants who settled rurally may have been able to erect shrines on their country property but crowded cities brought their own challenges. The ancient history of Christianity in Poland and purpose and meaning of roadside shrines did not, could not, take hold in urban America in the same way as it did in Poland. America was predominantly a Protestant country. The country was growing, defining itself, the cities filling with people of all faiths and origins, and anti-immigrant sentiment was a real presence. The climate of the new country and its industrial cities was just too different, provided too many challenges to contend with to provide the soil necessary for its growth. The spirit of one country cannot easily be transplanted to another country.

To be sure, crosses and figures of saints were established on church grounds and entrances to cemeteries in urban Polish-American communities throughout the United States, as they were in Poland. The city streets with their public, concrete sidewalks were not amenable to putting up a shrine to one of the saints in thanksgiving or supplication. They had to adapt and alter their practices. One way, perhaps, was to erect a shrine within the privacy of their own home. Home altars, with figures and images of the saints was a common practice in Poland as well but perhaps took on more significance in the new country. It established a holy place within the home and became a public symbol of their faith to all who visited the home. A carver of such shrines was Jan Dernoga (1894-1972). His parents immigrated from Poland and settled in Baltimore in the 1880s. He was born in the old section of Baltimore called Fels Point with all its shipbuilding and canneries. Like his father before him, Jan was a gifted wood carver. About *kapliczki* he wrote:

Wood carver Jan Dernoga on front steps of his home in Westport, south Baltimore, 1956.
Photo credit: Carla Hazard Tomaszewski

In Poland, nearly every Catholic home had a corner set aside for an altar with an icon or a kapliczka. They were decorated with live

Shrine carved by Jan Dernoga hanging in his granddaughters house.
Photo credit: Carla Hazard Tomaszewski

Close up of Dernoga shrine (opposite page) documenting its creation on the occasion of Poland's Millenium of Christianity. Photo credit: Carla Hazard Tomaszewski

flowers in summer and fall, or artificial flowers in winter. They were lighted with homemade pure wax candles and they had a fancy cut-glass dish with holy water and a home-made sprinkler. Some of these icons were very fancy. I remember my father worked a whole month on one. He had every square inch of it decorated. He made several – each one different. The pictures most commonly used were Our Lady of Częstochowa, Our Lady of Perpetual Help, Our Lady of Ostrobramska. The Hazard family have one of Our Lady of Perpetual Help. My wife has one of Our Lady of Częstochowa, in remembrance of the Polish Millennium of Christianity. (1966)

That cherished shrine now hangs in the home of his granddaughter, artist and author Carla Hazard Tomaszewski who recalls spending "long, full, wonderful weekends at our grandparent's house, helping them in the bakery and playing in dziadzi's basement woodshop."

Another adaptation that may have evolved in other urban cities as well but documented by historical photographs in Baltimore was a type of "window" shrine. Inside the windows facing the sidewalk and street there was the custom of placing holy pictures and figures of saints and the Blessed Virgin Mary for passers-by to see. Carla Hazard Tomaszewski remembers "starched curtains and crocheted doilies for the holy figures, artificial flowers and sometimes a fern."

Window shrine on St. Anne Street, Fels Point, Baltimore, MD.
Photo courtesy of Edith and Claire Pula, 2022.

A *New York Times* article dated April 1989, titled "Baltimore's Working Waterfront," referring to Fels Point, reads "… many homes boast shrines to the Blessed Virgin or Elvis in the windows."

It is my contention that once Polish Americans were able to leave the cities and purchase a home with an attached piece of property it became possible for them to think about erecting a shrine in the manner of their ancestors. Instead of erecting them at the roadside to mark the boundaries of their village or a place to bury their unshriven dead as was the custom in Poland, many Polish Americans erect

Close up of window in the front of Mary Kujawa's house in Canton, MD, 1979.
Photo credit: Elinor Cahn East Baltimore Documentary Photography Project Collection, The Photography Collections, University of Maryland, Baltimore County.

William Pulalski's Christmas window at his house on Bank Street, Balitmore, MD, 1977. Photo credit: Elinor Cahn East Baltimore Documentary Photography Project Collection, The Photography Collections, University of Maryland, Baltimore County, Tomaszewski

shrines in the privacy of their property for their own private reasons and as expressions of their faith. Jan Dernoga, mentioned above, made a shrine with a crucifix of his own carving for his daughter Stella (Stanisława) Dernoga Hazard. Stella's daughter, Carla, states "we lived in the suburbs with a nice back yard. Originally it was placed under the willow tree and he [grandfather] made it with a wooden 'table' to hold bird seed. She painted a picture of it titled 'Tree of Life.' Later mom moved it to the head of her rose bush garden." I am convinced that there are many, many such stories waiting to be told, collected and added to the scholarship of Polish-American studies.

Over the years, with more say in local and state governments, Polish Americans also began erecting shrines in public places to honor the history of Poland and these can be seen frequently in the cityscapes containing large populations of Polish Americans.

Crucifix carved by Jan Dernoga. Photo credit: *Carla Hazard Tomaszewski*

Painting titled "Tree of Life" by Stella Dernoga Hazard of cross and shrine made by her father, Jan Dernoga. Photo credit: Carla Hazard Tomaszewski

Shrine with Sorrowing Christ located at Veteran's plot at St. Stanislaus Cemetery, Cheektowaga, NY. The shrine was restored by Henry Swiatek (above) of Swiatek Studios prior to its rededication in 2021.
Photo credit:
Andrew Golebiowski

There is a World War II memorial shrine created at St. Stanislaus Cemetery in Buffalo, NY, in the early 1970s. The memorial was created in the shape of a Polish roadside shrine by renowned artist Józef Sławinski, who was a member Poland's Home Army during World War II. The Sorrowing Christ stands watch over the graves of Polish-born survivors of World War II who settled in the Buffalo, New York, area after the war. The artist is buried there as well. The inscription below the stained-glass image of Christ the King with two white eagles on either side reads: "They rest in eternal sleep dreaming of their homeland."

Cross called Golgotha Memorial on the grounds of St. Casimir's Church in Buffalo (Kaisertown), New York. Erected in 2019 on the 80th anniversary of World War II and dedicated in memory of lives lost in Poland. Photo credit: Sophie Hodorowicz Knab

Zakopane Chapel at Turners Falls, MA, dedicated to Mary, Queen of the Polish Martyrs of World War II, honoring the 108 Polish Martyrs canonized by Pope John Paul II in 1999. Photo credit: Rev. Charles Jan Di Mascola, Pastor Emeritus, Our Lady of Czestochowa Church, Turners Falls, MA

The Zakopane Chapel in Turners Falls, Massachusetts, is a work of love. Built in the style of the wooden architecture of the mountain region of Poland, the chapel was built and completely funded by an 88-year-old parishioner named Lawrence Krejmas as a labor of love and devotion. The cemetery shrine was modeled after the chapel of the Sacred Heart of Jesus in Jaszczurowka in Poland's Tatra Mountains. The chapel is dedicated to Mary, Queen of the Polish Martyrs of World War II, honoring the 108 Polish martyrs beatified and canonized by Pope John Paul II in 1999.

The following are a a few examples of personal, private shrines in the Western New York area:

Shrine dedicated to Our Lady of Częstochowa erected in 2010 at home of Steve and Diane Woloszyn, Delevan, New York.
Photo credit: Diane Woloszyn

Private backyard shrine devoted to Our Lady of Częstochowa, Cheektowaga, NY, erected 2008. *Photo credit: Sophie Hodorowicz Knab*

And finally, there is my backyard shrine. As an immigrant child, my parents struggled to give me a better life in America. I grew up in the Catholic faith and the traditions of my ancestors. I received an education. I worked and became a contributing member of society. Good health was mine. Family and friends were, and still are, treasures. Prayers were answered. And so as my ancestors did before me, the shrine was erected in thanksgiving for all the gifts received.

Shrine in my backyard erected as shrine of thanksgiving, 2005.
Photo credit: Sophie Hodorowicz Knab

BIBLIOGRAPHY

Adalberg, Samuel. *Księga przysłów, przypowieści i wyrażeń przysłowiowych Polskich* [Book of Polish proverbs, parables and conventional sayings]. Warszawa: Drukarnia Emila Skiwskiego, 1888-1894.

Bajek, Zofia and Mariusz Bajek. *Perełki Architektury: Kapliczki okolic Stalowa Woli* [Architectural Gems: Shrines in the Vicinity of Stalowa Wola]. Stalowa Wola: Wydawnictwo SZTAFETA, 2005.

Chętnik, Adam. *Kalendarzyk zwyczajów dorocznych, obrzędów i niektórych wierzeń ludu kurpiowskiego* [Calendar of annual customs, rituals and some beliefs of the Kurpie people]. Nowogród: Nakładem Muzeum Kurpiowskiego Polskiego Towarzystwo w Nowogrodzie, 1934.

_____. "Krzyże i Kapliczki Kurpiowskie" [Crosses and Shrines in Kurpie Region]. *Polska Sztuka Ludowa*, 1977, Nr.1, pp. 39-52.

Cieśla-Reinfussowa, Zofia. "Wystawa Sztuki Ludowej Województwa Lubelskiego" [Exhibition of Folk Art of the Lubelskie Voivodeship]. *Polska Sztuka Ludowa*, 1952, Nr. 2, pp. 100-102.

Czerwiński, Tomasz. *Kapliczki i krzyże przydrożne w Polsce* [Roadside shrines and crosses in Poland]. Warszawa: Sport i Turystyka – MUZA SA., 2012.

Dekowski, Jan Piotr. *"Przydrożne Kapliczki Słupowe w Południowo-wschodnej części województwo Łódzkiego"* [Roadside Shrines on columns in the South-Eastern part of the Łódź Province]. Prace i Materiały Muzeum Archeologicznego i Etnograficznego w Łodzi. Seria etnograficzna, Nr. 9, Łódź, 1965.

Fryś-Pietraszkowa, Anna Kunczyńska-Iracka and Marian Pokropek. *Sztuka Ludowa w Polsce* [Folk Art in Poland]. Warszawa: Wydawnictwo Arkady, 1988.

Galant, Ks. Dr. Wojciech. *Skarbiec Świętych Pańskich* [Treasury of Saints]. Milwaukee, Wisconsin: Diederich-Schafer Company, 1909.

Galicka, Izabella and Hanna Sygietynska. *"Chrystus Frasobliwy z Anielowa"* [The Sorrowing Christ from Anielowa]. *Polska Szutka Ludowa*, Nr. 2,1967, pp.109-110.

Gloger, Zygmunt. *Encyklopedia Starapolska. Tom I, II, III, IV.* [Encyclopedia of Old Poland. Volumes I - IV]. Warszawa: Wiedza Powszechna, 1985.

Groborz-Mazanek, Żaneta. *Kapliczki, Krzyże i figury Przydrożne Gminy Tarnowiec* [Chapels, crosses and roadside figures of the Tarnowiec Municipality]. Kraków: Oficyna Wydawnicza "APLA" 2002.

Jackowski, Aleksander. "Współczesna Rzeźba Zwana Ludowa" [Contemporary Folk Sculpture]. *Polska Sztuka Ludowa*, Nr.3-4, 1976.

Janicka-Krzywda, Urszula. *Kapliczki i Krzyze Przydrozne Polskiego Podkarpacia* [The Roadside Shrines and Crosses of Subcarpathia]. Warszawa: Towarzystwo Karpackie, 1991.

Jaskulanka, Paulina. *Kronika Okupacyjna Klasztoru Sióstr Urszulanek w Sieradzu* [Chronicles of the Convent of the Ursuline Sisters in Sieradz during the Occupation]. Częstochowa: Święty Paweł, 2017.

Kawałko, Danuta. "*Kaplice na Źródłach*" [Chapels on Springs]. *Zamojski Kwartalnik Kultury*, 2006, Nr.1-2, pp. 51-61.

Kolberg, Oskar. *LUD. Jego zwyczaje, sposób życia, mowa, podania, przysłowia, obrzędy, gusła, zabawy, pieśni, muzyka i tance. Krakowski I* [The People: Their traditions, manner of living, speech, proverbs, customs, witchcraft, entertainment, songs, music and dance. Kraków I]. Krakow: Polskie Towarszystwo Ludoznawcze, w drukarni Uniwersystetu Jagiiellonskiego, 1871-1890.

Kolinski, Dennis. "Shrines and Crosses in Rural Central Wisconsin." *Polish American Studies*, Vol.51, Autumn 1994. pp. 33-47.

Kowalski, Marek. *Śladami Świątków* [In the Footsteps of Roadside Saints]. Warszawa: Ludowa Spółdzielna Wydawnicza, 1971.

_____. *Sztuka Frasobliwa* [The Sorrowing Christ in Art]. Warszawa: Ludowa Spółdzielnia Wydawnicza, 1988.

Krasuski, W. "Krzyże i Kapliczki Przydrożne jako znak Podziału przestrstrzeni" [Roadside crosses and shrines as a sign of the division of space]. *Polska Sztuka Ludowa*, Nr.3-4, 1986.

Kunczyńska, Anna. "*Chrystus Frasobliwy w Polskiej Rzeźbie Ludowej*" [The Sorrowing Christ in Polish Folk Art.]. *Polska Sztuka Ludow*a, Nr.4, 1960, pp. 211-217.

Kunczyńska-Iracka, Anna. "*Chrystus Frasobliwy i Jego Miejsce w Tradycyjnej Religijności Ludowej*" [The Sorrowing Christ and His Place in Traditional Folk Religiosity]. *Polska Sztuka Ludowa*, Nr. 1, 1980, pp. 143-152.

_____. "*Krzyże Rzeźbione i Monolityczne Figury Drewniane z Małoposki*." [Carved crosses and monolithic wooden figures from Lesser Poland]. *Polska Sztuka Ludowa*, Nr. 3-4, 1976, pp. 181-198.

Kutrzeba-Pojarowa, Anna. "*Na Początki były Kapliczki*" [In the Beginning there were Roadside Shrines]. *Polska Sztuka Ludowa*, Nr.1-4, 1987, pp. 23-34.

Laskowski, W.S. "*Kult Św. Mikołaja w Polsce*" [The Cult of St. Nicholas in Poland]. *Ziemia*, Nr. 2, 1928, pp. 28-32.

Łopatkiewicz, Tadeusz. "*Ośrodki Kamieniarstwa Ludowego na Łemkowszczyźnie Środkowej*" [Centers of Folk Stonework in Lemko Region]. Polska *Sztuka Ludowa*, Nr.3-4, 1985, pp. 177-186.

Bibliography

Marczakowa, Krystyna. *"Kamieniarstwo Ludowe u Łemków"* [Folk Stonework among the Lemko]. *Polska Sztuka Ludowa*, Nr. 2, 1964, pp. 84-91.

Olędzki, Jacek. *"Artystyczna twórczość kowalska na terenie Kurpiowskij Puszczy Zielona od końca XIX w. do I Wojny Światowej"* [Artistic Blacksmithwork in the Kurpie Green Forest from the end of the 19th century to the First World War]. *Polska Sztuka Ludowa*, Nr. 4, 1961, pp. 199-214.

Piłsudski, Bronisław. *Krzyże Litewskie* [Lithuanian Crosses]. Kraków: Nakładem Redakcji "Orlego Lotu." Nr. 3, 1922 (digital version).

Piwocki, Ksawery. "Rzeźba Ludowa" [Folk Sculpture]. *Polska Sztuka Ludowa*, Nr. 3-4, 1976, pp. 131-150.

Polkowski, Franciszek. *Krzyże na Litwie* [Crosses in Lithuania]. Kraków: Materiały Wydawnictwo Towarzystwa "Polska Sztuka Stosowana" w Krakowie, Zeszyt XII, 1909 (digital version).

Pylak, B., and C. Krakowiak, eds., *Niepokalana. Kult Matki Bożej na ziemiach polskich w XIX wieku* [Immaculate: The Cult of the Mother of God on Polish lands in the 19th century]. Lublin: Redakcja Wydawnictw Kul, 1988.

Reinfuss, Roman. *"Rzeźba figuralna Łemków (Ze studiow nad ludowa rzeźba kamienną na Łemkowszczyźnie, cz.II"* [Figure Carvings of the Lemko (from the studies of folk stone carvings in Lemko region), Part II]. *Polska Sztuka Ludowa*, 1963, Nr. 3/4, pp. 122-134 (digital version).

_____. *"Ludowa Rzeżba Kamienna na Zachodnim Pogórze"* [Folk Sculpture in the Western Foothills]. *Polska Sztuka Ludowa*, 1976, pp. 167-180.

Reymont, Władysław. *The Peasants: Spring*. Alfred A. Knopf, 1925. Translated by Michael H. Dziewicki.

Seweryn, Tadeusz. *Kapliczki i Krzyże Przydrożne w Polsce* [Roadside Shrines and Crosses in Poland]. Warszawa: Instytut Wydawniczy PAX, 1958.

Swieży, Janusz. "*Świątkarze Biłgorajscy*" [Holy image makers in Biłgoraj]. *Polska Sztuka Ludowa*, 1947, Nr.1-2, pp. 50-54.

Szukiewicz, Wandalin "*Krzyże zdobne w Guberni Wileńskiej*" [Decorated Crosses in Vilnius Governorate]. *Wisła: Miesięcznik geograficzny-etnograficzny*, 1903, T.XVII, z.6, p. 699.

Taroni, Feliks. "*Kapliczki i krzyze przydrożne na Spisz*" [Roadside shrines and Crosses in Spisz]. *Lud*, 1906, pp. 161-170.

Załęski, Wojciech. "*Kapliczki Błagalne i Swięte Sosny z Okolic Supraśla*" [Shrines of Supplication and Sacred Pines in the Region of Supraśl]. *Polska Sztuka Ludowa*, R.42, Nr.3, 1988, pp. 186-195, 213-214.

Zielińska, Marta. *Kapliczki Warszawy* [Shrines of Warsaw]. Warszawa: Wydawnictwo Naukowe PWN, 1991.

Zin, Wiktor, Wojciech Oczkowski, Szymon Zin. *Opowieści o Polskich Kapliczkach* [Stories of Polish Shrines]. Wrocław: Zakład Narodowy im. Ossolińskich Wydawnictwo, 1995.

Żiwirska, Maria. *"Wincenty Kitowski. Iłżecki artysta ceramika"* [Vincent Kitowski: Ceramic artist from Iłża]. *Polska Sztuka Ludowa*, 1952, Nr.2, pp. 92-99.

INTERNET SOURCES:

https://suchainfo.pl

http://www.mojewojennedziecinstwo.pl/pdf/03_banek_mojdom. pdf

http://kapliczki.org.pl/kapliczki/Kapliczki,_krzy%C5%BCe_i_ figury_przydro%C5%BCne

http://polskaniezwykla.pl

https://www.konskie.org.pl

https://www.mnw.art.pl

https://etnomuzeum.eu

https://www.swietyjozef.kalisz.pl

https://www.szukajwarchiwach.gov.pl/en/web/narodowe-archiwum-cyfrowe

INDEX

relics, origin of use of, 75
Robbers Chapel, Zawoj Policzna, 47
Rogation Days, 129-131
roosters on crosses, use of, 120
Russian purge of Marian images, 73-74
Rzeszów, Poland, 67, 108

Sacred Heart devotions, 137
salt mine legend, 86. *See also* Wieliczka Salt Mine
Sandomierz, Poland, 65, 98
Sanok school of woodcarving, 108
sheet metal, use of for shrines, 117
shrines, blessing/preserving/decorating of, 123-127, 133-134
shrines, meaning/importance of for villagers, 122-123, 145-152
shrines against evil, 38-41
shrines of penance, 45-47
shrines of remembrance, 48, 54
shrines of supplication, 44
shrines of thanksgiving, 41-44, 56
Sieradz, Poland, in WWII, 59-61
Silesia (Upper and Lower), Poland, 22, 23, 45
Skulsk, Poland, 116
Sławinski, Józef, 163
Sorrowing Christ figures, 64-67, 104, 108-109, 116
Stachowicz, Theodor Baltazar (artist), 25
Stalowa Wola, Poland, shrine of thanksgiving in, 42-43
St. Adalbert, 6, 98
St. Anthony of Padua, 96-97
St. Barbara, 87-88
St. Bartholomew, 99
St. Felicity, chapel of, 42-43
St. Florian, 88-90, 98
St. Francis of Assisi, 98
St. Francis Xavier, 98
St. Giles, 99
St. Hedwig, 82-83
St. Isidor the Plowman, 99, 130
St. John Nepomucen, 79-82
St. Joseph, 76-79
St. Joseph of Kalisz, 76-77

About the Author

Sophie Hodorowicz Knab is a noted Polish-American lecturer and author whose books include *Polish Customs, Traditions & Folklore, Polish Herbs, Flowers & Folk Medicine, Polish Country Kitchen Cookbook, and Wearing the Letter P: Polish Women as Forced Laborers in Nazi Germany,* all published by Hippocrene Books. She is a contributor to the Polish American Journal and the AmPol Eagle newspapers. She resides in Grand Island, New York. Read more on Polish traditions, culture and history at SophieKnab.com

Also by Sophie Hodorowicz Knab ...

Polish Herbs, Flowers & Folk Medicine

"Filled with illustrations and fascinating information, Polish Herbs, Flowers & Folk Medicine *is a veritable treasure trove of history, how-to, and inspiration."*

—The Midwest Book Review

Taking the reader on a historical tour of herbs and flowers used in Poland throughout the centuries, this carefully-researched volume captures the unique history and role of plant life once essential to the people of Poland. Wander through mon- astery, castle and cottage gardens with acclaimed Polish-American author Sophie Hodorowicz Knab as she explores the growth of medi- cine and pharmacies and provides information on the use of over 100 plants, used in healing as well as in daily life and seasonal holidays throughout the year.

ISBN 978-0-7818-1414-0 • paperback and e-book available

Polish Customs, Traditions & Folklore

"A richly detailed and well-informed month-by month accounting of all the major Polish customs and traditions practiced over the centuries. Ms. Knab stirs and reawakens our ancestral memory."

—The Kosciuszko Foundation Newsletter

This unique, well-researched reference is arranged by month, showing the various occasions, feasts and holidays prominent in Polish culture—beginning with December it continues through Holy Week Cus- toms, superstitions, beliefs and rituals associated with farming, Pente- cost, Corpus Christi, midsummer, harvest festival, wedding rites, Name Days, birth and death. Line illustrations throughout enrich this varied treasury of Polish folklore and the revised edition includes a chapter on "Traditional Polish Games and Pastimes for Children."

ISBN 978-0-7818-0515-5 • hardcover

The Polish Country Kitchen Cookbook

"…blends recipes for favorite Polish foods with the history and culture which created them, using seasonal arrangement to explore Polish life and how food traditions evolved. Recipes have been adapted for American kitchens but retain their authentic roots, while plenty of Polish cultural insights make for inviting leisure browsing by more than just the cook."

—*The Midwest Book Review*

This popular cookbook by beloved Polish-American author Sophie Hodorowicz Knab combines more than 100 recipes for favorite Polish foods with the history and cultural traditions that created them. Arranged according to the cycle of seasons, it explores life in the Polish countryside through the year and gives readers priceless historical information and insightful answers to common questions (like the meaning behind the Pascal butter lamb) asked by descendants of Polish immigrants. It has been updated with a section on Polish Feasts & Festivals. Lovely illustrations and pearls of practical wisdom ("Household Hints") from the old Polish kitchen marvelously complement this book.

ISBN 978-0-7818-1294-8 • paperback

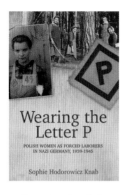

Wearing the Letter P: Polish Women as Forced Laborers in Nazi Germany, 1939-1945

"My mother, who was a Polish forced laborer from 1942 to 1945, never talked to me about her life during the war. Now I know. With a great combination of scholarly research and moving first person accounts, Knab's Wearing the Letter P *vividly describes the terrible, heartbreaking ordeal that my mother and hundreds of thousands of Poles suffered. She expertly sheds light on a part of World War II that's been totally ignored."*

—Charles Belfoure, author of *The Paris Architect*

In this unflinching, detailed portrait of a forgotten group of Nazi forced labor survivors, author Sophie Horodowicz Knab reveals the personal stories of hundreds of Polish women who were forced to leave their homes to work in Nazi German factories and farms during World War II. From sexual assault, starvation, and illness to tremendous physical and psychological trauma, the atrocities these women suffered have never been fully explored until now.

Knab explains how it all happened, from the beginning of Nazi occupation in Poland to liberation: the roundups; the horrors of transit camps; the living and working conditions of Polish women in agriculture and industry; and the anguish of sexual exploitation and forced abortions—all under the constant threat of concentration camps. Knab draws from documents, government and family records, rare photos, and most importantly, numerous victim accounts and diaries, letters and trial testimonies, finally giving these women a voice and bringing to light the atrocities that they endured.

ISBN 978-0-7818-1359-4 • paperback and e-book available

POLISH INTEREST TITLE

FOOTPRINTS OF
POLONIA
Polish
Historical Sites
Across
North America

Edited by Ewa E. Barczyk

**Footprints of Polonia:
Polish Historical Sites Across
North America**

Edited by Ewa E. Barczyk

"*Footprints of Polonia is an outstanding look at
the way that Polish Americans have transformed
America's cities, suburbs, and towns. It is an essential
guide to the physical impact of one of the country's
largest ethnic groups.*"

—Dominic A. Pacyga, author of
*American Warsaw: The Rise, Fall, and Rebirth of
Polish Chicago*

The innumerable contributions of Polish immigrants and their descendants on communities in North America can be seen on monuments, bridges, churches, cultural centers, and cemeteries across the continent. These "footprints" of Polonia (the Polish diaspora), commemorating towering events and figures from history that are a source of pride among Polish Americans, are cataloged for readers in this unique volume. From Revolutionary War heroes Tadeusz Kosciuśzko and Casimir Pulaski to more recent figures like Pope John Paul II and political movements like Solidarity, statues and historic sites all over North America pay homage to their contributions and importance.

This project is based on the input of volunteers from Polish organizations all over North America, who helped identify the most important sites in their region and provided summaries and pictures for over 200 entries. The guide is organized alphabetically by states and provinces, with entries that describe the historical significance of each site. Most entries also include a color photo. Informative prefaces and introductions from the editor and other historians help contextualize the culture of Polish immigrants and their deep, lasting connection to Poland.

Footprints of Polonia can serve as the perfect travel companion for anyone who wants to learn about the rich history and heritage of the Polish diaspora. It is also an excellent resource for Polish language schools and Polish American organizations who want to learn more about and take pride in sites of interest in their area.

ISBN 978-0-7818-1435-5 • paperback